AI INCOME REVOLUTION

Unleashing Google Gemini AI for Passive Income Mastery: A Comprehensive Guide to Automate Your Wealth, Dominate Your Niche and Achieve Financial Freedom

Tech Talker

Table of contents

Introduction

Welcome to the future of income generation—welcome to the AI Income Revolution. In the realm of passive income, where dreams of financial freedom converge with the relentless pursuit of innovation, a groundbreaking force has emerged: Google Gemini AI.

As we embark on this transformative journey together, envision a world where the intricate dance between artificial intelligence and your aspirations harmoniously leads to a steady stream of automated wealth. This guide is more than a manual; it's an invitation to revolutionize your approach to income and embrace the power of Google Gemini AI.

In the chapters that follow, we will unravel the intricacies of Gemini AI—unleashing its prowess in natural language processing, machine learning, and data analysis. From content creation to customer service excellence, from digital marketing optimization to the creation of online courses, Gemini AI stands as your ally in the pursuit of financial success.

This isn't just a guide; it's a roadmap to $1,000 a month and beyond. It's a blueprint for dominating your chosen niche and achieving a level of financial autonomy that transcends the conventional 9-to-5 grind. The strategies we explore aren't mere theories; they are the gateway to a realm where passive income is no longer a distant ideal but a tangible reality.

In the subsequent chapters, we'll delve into the intricacies of leveraging Gemini AI for content creation and monetization, optimizing your e-commerce ventures, and crafting marketing campaigns that resonate in a digitally evolved landscape. We'll navigate the challenges of maintaining authenticity, staying ethically aligned, and thriving in a potentially saturated market.

But this journey extends beyond the basics. We'll explore additional income streams—selling code snippets, venturing into creative writing, and offering data analysis and reporting services. The tips for success shared herein aren't just principles; they're the compass guiding you through the dynamic landscape of Gemini AI.

As we conclude this introduction, consider this your initiation into a community of forward-thinkers and innovators. This isn't just a guide; it's an immersive experience. The AI Income Revolution awaits, and you stand at the forefront. Let's uncover the limitless potential of Google Gemini AI together and witness your income streams ascend towards the coveted $1,000 a month goal.

Buckle up—your future of automated income and financial freedom begins now.

Chapter 1:

Unlocking the Power of Google Gemini AI

Understanding Gemini AI

In the realm of revolutionary technologies, Google Gemini AI emerges as a powerhouse, seamlessly integrating three pivotal capabilities that redefine the landscape of income generation: natural language processing, machine learning, and data analysis.

Natural Language Processing (NLP)

Imagine an artificial intelligence system that not only comprehends human language but interprets its nuances, context, and intricacies. Google Gemini AI, with its advanced NLP capabilities, transcends mere understanding. It dives into the essence of language, deciphering meanings, sentiments, and intents with remarkable accuracy.

This NLP prowess opens the door to unparalleled content creation. It enables the generation of human-like text, ensuring that the automated output isn't just coherent but resonates with the intricacies of language. Blog posts, articles, and marketing content become not just pieces of information but compelling narratives crafted by the sophistication of Gemini AI.

Machine Learning Mastery

Beyond understanding language, Gemini AI embraces the realm of machine learning—a dynamic process where it learns, evolves, and adapts based on patterns and experiences. This transformative capability empowers the system to continuously enhance its performance, fine-tune its responses, and adapt to the ever-shifting landscape of user interactions.

In the context of passive income, machine learning becomes the driving force behind predictive analytics. Gemini AI doesn't just respond; it anticipates. It understands user behaviors, predicts market trends, and optimizes content creation and marketing strategies to align with the evolving preferences of your audience.

Data Analysis at its Core

At the core of Gemini AI's capabilities lies a robust foundation in data analysis. It doesn't merely process information; it dissects it, derives insights, and transforms raw data into actionable intelligence. This analytical prowess extends far beyond the realms of content creation, infiltrating every facet of passive income generation.

Market trends, consumer behaviors, and performance metrics become the canvas upon which Gemini AI paints the picture of financial success. By harnessing the power of data analysis, this AI system doesn't just operate in the present; it strategically positions you for the future. It's the compass guiding your choices, ensuring that every move is calculated, optimized, and poised for success.

In essence, Google Gemini AI doesn't merely process information; it comprehends, learns, and strategizes. It's not just a tool;

it's a partner in your journey to automated income. The convergence of natural language processing, machine learning, and data analysis sets the stage for a revolution—a revolution that propels you toward the pinnacle of passive income mastery.

Its transformative applications

Google Gemini AI isn't just an artificial intelligence system—it's a transformative force reshaping the landscape of digital marketing, content creation, and customer service. Let's delve into the profound impact it has across these pivotal domains:

Digital Marketing Evolution: In the realm of digital marketing, where precision and relevance are paramount, Gemini AI emerges as a game-changer. Its data analysis capabilities empower marketers to dissect market trends, consumer behaviors, and campaign performance with unprecedented accuracy. No longer bound by conventional strategies, digital marketers can optimize their campaigns dynamically, ensuring that every advertising dollar spent yields maximum returns.

Gemini AI's ability to analyze vast datasets allows for the identification of subtle patterns and trends that might elude human observation. This not only refines the targeting of ads but also enhances the overall efficiency of digital marketing efforts. Whether it's crafting personalized content, predicting consumer preferences, or fine-tuning ad placements, Gemini AI becomes the strategic ally in navigating the complex landscape of digital advertising.

Revolutionizing Content Creation: Content is the lifeblood of the online world, and Google Gemini AI injects a new dimension into its creation. Imagine a tool that not only generates content but understands the nuances of language, tailoring its output to captivate and engage. Gemini AI, with its natural language processing capabilities, takes content creation beyond mere information dissemination—it crafts narratives that resonate with human emotions.

From blog posts to social media updates, the content produced by Gemini AI isn't just algorithmic; it's infused with the essence of human-like expression. It adapts its tone, style, and structure to align with the desired audience, ensuring that the message isn't just conveyed but embraced. The result is a library of content that transcends the limitations of automation—it connects, inspires, and establishes a genuine rapport with the audience.

Elevating Customer Service Excellence: In the realm of customer service, where responsiveness and efficiency are the cornerstones of success, Gemini AI takes center stage. Its chatbot capabilities enable businesses to offer 24/7 customer support without the constraints of human availability. This not only enhances customer satisfaction but also contributes to the seamless progression of sales and support processes.

Gemini AI's chatbots aren't just automated responders; they are intelligent conversationalists. They understand user queries, provide relevant information, and can even anticipate needs based on historical interactions. This level of sophistication doesn't replace human touch but augments it, ensuring that customer service becomes a strategic asset rather than a logistical challenge.

In essence, Google Gemini AI doesn't just augment processes—it transforms them. In digital marketing, it becomes the architect of precision campaigns; in content creation, it evolves into the curator of compelling narratives; and in customer service, it stands as the ambassador of seamless interactions. The applications of Gemini AI are not confined to tasks; they redefine the benchmarks of excellence across the digital landscape.

Expanding Passive Income Horizons

At the core of financial independence lies the concept of passive income—a paradigm where earnings flow in without direct, active involvement. It's the embodiment of the dream to escape the confines of a traditional 9-to-5, creating avenues for wealth generation that transcend the limitations of time and effort. As we navigate the realms of passive income, Google Gemini AI emerges as the catalyst, expanding the spectrum of opportunities with unparalleled ingenuity.

The Essence of Passive Income

Passive income is not merely a monetary stream; it's a philosophy that reshapes the traditional notions of work and income. It's the art of creating systems and assets that work tirelessly on your behalf, generating revenue even when you're not directly engaged. From rental properties and dividends to online businesses and investments, passive income represents the ultimate pursuit of financial autonomy.

The allure of passive income lies in its potential to break free from the shackles of a linear income model. Instead of exchanging time for money in a conventional job, passive income allows individuals to leverage their resources, knowledge, and creativity to build income streams that persist, evolve, and multiply over time.

Gemini AI's Role in Expanding Opportunities

Enter Google Gemini AI—a technological marvel that doesn't just align with the principles of passive income; it elevates them to unprecedented heights. By harnessing the capabilities of natural language processing, machine learning, and data analysis, Gemini AI becomes the conduit through which passive income opportunities flourish.

1. **Content Creation Revolutionized:** Gemini AI becomes the wordsmith, creating content that not only resonates with audiences but also ranks high in search engines. This content, infused with the essence of human-like expression, becomes the cornerstone of

blogs, websites, and social media platforms. The result is a continuous flow of traffic, engagement, and, ultimately, passive income through avenues like affiliate marketing, ad revenue, and sponsored content.

2. **E-Commerce and Customer Service Enhancement:** For those venturing into e-commerce, Gemini AI's chatbots stand as the 24/7 customer service representatives. Beyond mere automation, they become the bridge that enhances customer experience, drives sales, and contributes to passive income. With streamlined customer interactions, businesses not only thrive but do so without the need for constant manual intervention.

3. **Optimized Digital Marketing Strategies:** In the realm of digital marketing, Gemini AI analyzes market trends, predicts consumer behavior, and optimizes advertising campaigns. This isn't just about selling products or services; it's about strategically positioning oneself in the digital space. The result is a more efficient allocation of resources, higher returns on investment, and the creation of a perpetual marketing engine that contributes to passive income.

In essence, Google Gemini AI doesn't just augment passive income opportunities; it orchestrates a symphony of possibilities. It's the virtuoso that transforms content into currency, customer interactions into revenue, and marketing efforts into perpetual streams of income. The spectrum of opportunities broadens, and the pursuit of financial freedom evolves into an intricate dance between innovation and income generation.

Examples showcasing the impact of Gemini AI on income streams

Real-world examples serve as powerful testaments to the tangible impact of Google Gemini AI on income streams. Let's explore scenarios where individuals and businesses have harnessed the transformative power of Gemini AI, leading to substantial and sustainable financial gains.

Example 1: E-Commerce Enchantment

Consider an e-commerce entrepreneur named Sarah who runs a small online store selling handmade jewelry. Sarah, aware of the challenges in providing 24/7 customer service, integrates Gemini AI's chatbot capabilities into her website. This strategic move transforms the customer experience. Potential buyers receive instant responses to inquiries, detailed product information, and personalized recommendations—all powered by Gemini AI.

The impact is two-fold. First, Sarah's customer satisfaction soars, contributing to increased sales and a growing customer base. Second, the automated nature of customer service allows Sarah to focus on expanding her product line, enhancing the uniqueness of her offerings, and exploring additional income streams. Gemini AI, in this scenario, becomes the cornerstone for passive income by optimizing the customer interaction process.

Example 2: Content Creation Mastery

Meet Alex, a blogger aspiring to monetize his platform through affiliate marketing and ad revenue. Aware of the importance of high-quality content, Alex leverages Gemini AI for content creation. The AI's natural language processing capabilities enable Alex to produce engaging, SEO-optimized articles at a pace that was previously unattainable.

As a result, Alex experiences a significant uptick in website traffic. The AI-generated content not only attracts a larger audience but also ranks well on search engines, enhancing the visibility of affiliate links and ads. The exponential growth in traffic transforms Alex's blog into a revenue-generating machine. Gemini AI, in this instance, becomes the driving force behind passive income through content that resonates and captivates.

Example 3: Marketing Mastery Unleashed

Enter David, a digital marketer navigating the competitive landscape of online advertising. With Gemini AI as his ally, David optimizes his marketing strategies with unparalleled precision. The AI's data analysis capabilities dissect market trends, consumer behavior, and campaign performance in real time.

David noticed a significant reduction in advertising costs while simultaneously witnessing a spike in conversions. Gemini AI's ability to adapt and learn from user interactions allows David to refine his targeting, ensuring that every ad reaches the most receptive audience. The result is a substantial increase in return on investment, catapulting David into a realm where his marketing efforts become not just an expense but a perpetual source of passive income.

These real-world examples showcase the transformative impact of Google Gemini AI on diverse income streams. From e-commerce and content creation to digital marketing, Gemini AI emerges as a catalyst that not only optimizes processes but fundamentally reshapes the dynamics of income generation. The stories of Sarah, Alex, and David underscore the versatility and efficacy of Gemini AI in turning innovative ideas into lucrative, sustainable realities.

Chapter 2:

Strategies for Passive Income with Gemini AI

Content Creation and Monetization

Unlocking the full potential of Google Gemini AI for content creation involves not just leveraging its capabilities but also understanding how to strategically harness its power to captivate your audience. Let's delve into content creation strategies that go beyond mere information dissemination, ensuring that the content generated resonates with and engages your audience on a profound level.

1. Understanding Your Audience: Before diving into content creation, it's essential to comprehend your target audience—their preferences, pain points, and interests. Gemini AI, with its data analysis capabilities, can help identify trends in consumer behavior, allowing you to tailor your content to precisely match what your audience is seeking.

2. Crafting Compelling Storytelling:

One of the most potent ways to captivate an audience is through storytelling. Gemini AI, infused with natural language processing, can craft narratives that evoke emotions and resonate with readers. Whether it's the story of your brand, the journey of a product, or a narrative that aligns with your niche, storytelling creates a connection that transcends conventional content.

3. Personalizing Content Experiences:

Gemini AI's ability to analyze user interactions opens the door to personalized content experiences. By understanding individual preferences, the AI can dynamically adjust content recommendations, ensuring that each user receives content tailored to their interests. This personalization not only enhances engagement but also fosters a sense of connection between the audience and your brand.

4. Creating Interactive Content: Engagement goes beyond passive consumption. Gemini AI can assist in creating interactive content such as quizzes, polls, and surveys. This not only keeps your audience actively involved but also provides valuable insights into their preferences. Interactive content becomes a two-way street, fostering a sense of participation and community.

5. Optimizing for SEO: Content creation isn't just about engaging your current audience; it's also about reaching new audiences. Gemini AI, with its SEO optimization capabilities, ensures that your content ranks well in search engines. This not only expands your reach but also attracts organic traffic—individuals actively seeking the information or products you offer.

6. Incorporating Visual Appeal: Gemini AI isn't limited to text; it can generate visually appealing content. Whether it's infographics, images, or even video scripts, the AI can ensure that your content is not only informative but also visually engaging. Visual appeal enhances the overall content experience and is crucial in capturing and retaining audience attention.

7. Staying Authentic and Genuine: While leveraging AI for content creation, it's essential to maintain authenticity. Ensure that the content generated aligns with your brand voice and values. Gemini AI is a tool, not a replacement for human creativity and intuition. Inject your personality into the content to establish a genuine connection with your audience.

In essence, the strategy to captivate your audience with Gemini AI involves a holistic approach that integrates data-driven insights, storytelling, personalization, interactivity, SEO optimization, visual appeal, and an unwavering commitment to authenticity. By strategically combining these elements, you can create content that not only captures attention but also fosters lasting connections with your audience.

Monetization avenues

Monetizing your content is a crucial step in turning the captivating material generated by Google Gemini AI into a sustainable income stream. Let's explore three powerful avenues—affiliate marketing, ad revenue, and sponsored content—and how to effectively integrate them into your content strategy.

1. Affiliate Marketing Mastery: Affiliate marketing is a dynamic strategy where you promote products or services, and in return, you earn a commission for each sale or action generated through your unique affiliate link.

Here's how to harness Google Gemini AI for affiliate marketing success:

- **Strategic Product Selection:** Utilize Gemini AI's data analysis capabilities to identify products or services that align with your audience's interests. Selecting products your audience is genuinely interested in increases the likelihood of conversions.

- **Seamless Integration of Affiliate Links:** Integrate affiliate links seamlessly into the content generated by Gemini AI. The key is to make these links a natural part of your narrative, ensuring they enhance the user experience rather than disrupt it.

- **Creating Compelling Reviews and Recommendations:** Leverage Gemini AI to craft compelling product reviews and recommendations. Humanize the content by sharing personal experiences and insights, making it more relatable to your audience.

2. Ad Revenue Optimization: Ad revenue, often generated through platforms like Google AdSense, involves displaying ads on your content-rich sites.

Here's how to optimize ad revenue with Gemini AI:

- **Content Layout for Ad Placement:** Utilize Gemini AI to analyze user behavior and optimize your content layout for strategic ad placement. This includes placing ads where they are more likely to attract attention without compromising the overall user experience.

- **Keyword Optimization for Ad Targeting:** Leverage Gemini AI's natural language processing to optimize your content for relevant keywords. This not only enhances your content's search engine visibility but also ensures more targeted ad placements.

- **Content Volume and Quality:** Use Gemini AI to maintain a consistent flow of high-quality content. Regular, engaging content attracts more traffic, increasing the opportunities for ad impressions and clicks.

3. Sponsored Content Success: Sponsored content involves partnering with brands to create content that aligns with their products or services. This can take the form of articles, videos, or social media posts.

Here's how to effectively integrate sponsored content:

- **Aligning Sponsored Content with Your Niche:** Leverage Gemini AI to ensure that sponsored content seamlessly aligns with your niche and resonates with your audience. Authenticity is key in maintaining trust with your followers.

- **Data-Driven Audience Insights:** Use Gemini AI's data analysis capabilities to gain insights into your audience's preferences. This data can be invaluable when tailoring sponsored content to match the specific interests of your audience.

- **Balancing Sponsored and Organic Content:** Strike a balance between sponsored and organic content. Too much sponsored content can be perceived as inauthentic, potentially alienating your audience. Gemini AI can assist in finding this equilibrium.

Incorporating these monetization strategies seamlessly into your content strategy, guided by the insights provided by Google Gemini AI, ensures that your income streams grow organically as your audience engages with your captivating and strategically monetized content.

E-Commerce and Customer Service Excellence

Elevating your e-commerce game with Gemini AI-driven 24/7 customer service involves leveraging the chatbot capabilities of Google Gemini AI to provide a seamless, responsive, and personalized customer experience.

Here's how you can integrate Gemini AI into your e-commerce customer service strategy:

1. Instant Response and Availability:

Gemini AI chatbots operate round the clock, ensuring that customers receive instant responses to their queries at any time of the day. This availability is a game-changer in the e-commerce landscape, where customers expect quick and efficient support.

2. Handling Basic Inquiries and Transactions: Gemini AI is equipped to handle a wide range of basic customer inquiries, from order status and product information to transaction processing. By automating routine tasks, your customer service team can focus on more complex issues, enhancing overall efficiency.

3. Personalized Recommendations: Utilize Gemini AI to provide personalized product recommendations based on customer preferences and purchase history. This enhances the customer experience by making their interactions with your e-commerce platform more tailored and relevant.

4. Order Tracking and Updates: Gemini AI can seamlessly integrate with your e-commerce system to provide real-time order tracking and updates. Customers can inquire about the status of their orders, receive shipping information, and stay informed throughout the entire purchasing process.

5. Problem Resolution and Escalation: While handling routine inquiries, Gemini AI can also identify more complex issues that require human intervention. The chatbot can efficiently escalate such matters to your customer service team, ensuring that problems are addressed promptly and effectively.

6. Feedback Collection and Improvement: Use Gemini AI to collect feedback from customers regarding their experience with your e-commerce platform. Analyzing this feedback can provide valuable insights into areas for improvement, helping you enhance your services and optimize the customer journey.

7. Integration with Multiple Channels: Gemini AI-driven customer service can seamlessly integrate with various communication channels, including your website, mobile app, and social media platforms. This ensures a consistent and unified customer experience across different touchpoints.

8. Language Understanding and Natural Interactions: Gemini AI's natural language processing capabilities allow it to understand customer inquiries in a conversational manner. This enhances the natural flow of interactions, making the customer service experience more user-friendly and engaging.

9. Cost Efficiency and Scalability: By automating routine customer service tasks, Gemini AI contributes to cost efficiency. It also offers scalability, allowing your e-commerce platform to handle a growing customer base without a proportional increase in customer service staffing.

10. Continuous Learning and Improvement: Gemini AI continuously learns from customer interactions, improving its responses and efficiency over time. This adaptability ensures that your e-commerce customer service remains dynamic and responsive to evolving customer needs.

In summary, integrating Gemini AI into your e-commerce customer service strategy transforms the way you interact with customers. The 24/7 availability, personalized interactions, and efficiency of the chatbot contribute to an elevated customer experience, fostering loyalty and satisfaction in the competitive e-commerce landscape.

Customer service excellence

Customer service excellence is not just about ensuring customer satisfaction; it's a strategic driver that can contribute significantly to passive income. Here's how delivering exceptional customer service goes beyond meeting immediate needs and becomes a catalyst for long-term financial success:

1. Building Customer Loyalty: Exceptional customer service builds trust and loyalty. Satisfied customers are more likely to become repeat buyers and advocates for your brand. Repeat business is a foundational element of passive income, as it establishes a consistent and reliable revenue stream without the need for constant acquisition efforts.

2. Word-of-Mouth Marketing: Satisfied customers are likely to share their positive experiences with others through word-of-mouth marketing. This organic form of promotion can lead to new customers discovering your business, contributing to organic growth and increased passive income.

3. Positive Online Reviews and Testimonials: Exceptional customer service often translates into positive online reviews and testimonials. Positive reviews not only attract new customers but also enhance your online reputation. A stellar reputation can drive organic traffic to your e-commerce platform, positively impacting your conversion rates and, consequently, passive income.

4. Reducing Returns and Refunds: When customers receive prompt and effective assistance, the likelihood of returns and refunds decreases. A lower rate of returns and refunds is crucial for maintaining healthy profit margins and sustaining passive income. Exceptional customer service helps address customer concerns before they escalate to the point of requiring a return.

5. Encouraging Upsells and Cross-Sells: A well-trained customer service team can identify opportunities for upselling or cross-selling additional

products or services. By providing
personalized recommendations and
addressing customer needs, you can
increase the average transaction value,
contributing to enhanced revenue and
potential passive income.

6. Enhancing Brand Reputation: A
positive customer service experience
contributes to a positive overall brand
reputation. A reputable brand attracts more
customers and can command premium
prices for products or services. This
enhanced brand value creates a foundation
for sustained passive income.

**7. Retaining Customers in a
Competitive Landscape:** In competitive
markets, customer service excellence

becomes a key differentiator. Customers are more likely to remain loyal to a brand that consistently provides exceptional service. Retaining customers in a competitive landscape is essential for building a stable and predictable passive income stream.

8. Increasing Customer Lifetime Value: Customer service excellence contributes to increasing the lifetime value of customers. Satisfied customers who continue to engage with your brand over an extended period contribute more to your overall revenue. Maximizing customer lifetime value is a fundamental aspect of passive income sustainability.

In essence, customer service excellence is a multifaceted strategy that extends beyond immediate satisfaction. It becomes a cornerstone for building lasting relationships, fostering positive word-of-mouth, and creating a brand that customers trust. As these elements align, they lay the groundwork for sustained passive income through repeat business, organic growth, and a positive brand image in the marketplace.

Digital Marketing Optimization

Leveraging Google Gemini AI to analyze market trends and consumer behavior can provide valuable insights that empower your business strategy. Here's how you can harness the capabilities of Gemini AI to gain a deeper understanding of market dynamics and consumer preferences:

1. Data-Driven Market Analysis: Gemini AI excels in processing vast amounts of data to identify patterns, trends, and anomalies. Utilize the AI to analyze market data, including competitor performance, industry trends, and emerging market segments. By synthesizing this information, you can make informed decisions about market entry, product positioning, and strategic partnerships.

2. Consumer Sentiment Analysis: Gemini AI's natural language processing capabilities enable it to analyze online conversations, reviews, and social media mentions to gauge consumer sentiment. This insight into how consumers feel about your brand, products, or industry can guide your marketing strategies, product development, and overall brand positioning.

3. Predictive Analytics for Demand Forecasting: By analyzing historical data and current market trends, Gemini AI can assist in predicting future demand for products or services. This predictive analytics capability allows you to optimize inventory management, anticipate market shifts, and stay ahead of consumer demand, contributing to more efficient operations and increased revenue.

4. Identifying Emerging Consumer Preferences: Keep a pulse on emerging consumer preferences and behaviors. Gemini AI can process large datasets to identify shifts in consumer preferences, helping your business adapt quickly to changing market dynamics. Whether it's a preference for sustainable products or a shift towards digital services, staying ahead of trends positions your business for success.

5. Competitor Benchmarking: Analyze the strategies and performance of your competitors using Gemini AI. The AI can provide insights into competitor advertising, customer engagement strategies, and product positioning. This information allows you to benchmark your business against industry leaders and identify areas for differentiation and improvement.

6. Optimizing Marketing Campaigns: Use Gemini AI to analyze the effectiveness of your marketing campaigns. The AI can assess audience engagement, conversion rates, and the impact of different marketing channels. By understanding what resonates with your target audience, you can optimize your marketing efforts for better returns on investment.

7. Customized Product Development:
Gemini AI's insights can guide product development by identifying gaps in the market or areas where consumer needs are not adequately addressed. Customizing products based on consumer preferences and market trends enhances the likelihood of success in the competitive landscape.

8. Dynamic Pricing Strategies: Analyze consumer behavior and market dynamics to implement dynamic pricing strategies. Gemini AI can assist in identifying optimal pricing points, responding to changes in consumer demand, and maximizing revenue through strategic pricing adjustments.

Incorporating Gemini AI insights into your market analysis and consumer behavior understanding equips your business with a competitive edge. The ability to make data-driven decisions, anticipate market shifts, and align your strategies with consumer preferences positions your business for sustained success in a dynamic and evolving marketplace.

Craft targeted digital marketing campaigns that optimize your advertising spend

Crafting targeted digital marketing campaigns with the assistance of Google Gemini AI can significantly optimize your advertising spend. Here's a strategic approach to ensure your campaigns are not only cost-effective but also yield higher returns on investment:

1. **Audience Segmentation and Persona Development:** Utilize Gemini AI to analyze user data and identify distinct audience segments based on demographics, behavior, and preferences. Develop detailed buyer personas for each segment to tailor your marketing messages effectively.

2. **Behavioral Targeting:** Leverage Gemini AI's ability to analyze user behavior to implement behavioral targeting in your campaigns. Tailor your ads based on users' online activities, such as their search history, website visits, and interactions with previous ads. This ensures that your ads reach users with a demonstrated interest in your products or services.

3. Dynamic Ad Personalization: Use Gemini AI to dynamically personalize your ads based on user data. This includes personalized product recommendations, dynamic pricing based on user behavior, and ad copy variations to suit different audience segments. Personalized ads have higher engagement rates and contribute to improved conversion rates.

4. Predictive Analytics for Campaign Optimization: Leverage Gemini AI's predictive analytics capabilities to forecast the performance of your digital marketing campaigns. This includes predicting click-through rates, conversion rates, and overall campaign success. By identifying potential challenges or opportunities in advance, you can optimize your campaign strategy before implementation.

5. Optimized Ad Placement: Gemini AI can analyze data to identify the most effective ad placements for your target audience. Whether it's selecting the right websites, social media platforms, or mobile apps, strategic ad placement ensures that your campaigns reach the right audience at the right time.

6. A/B Testing for Continuous Improvement: Implement A/B testing with the assistance of Gemini AI to experiment with different ad creatives, headlines, and calls-to-action. Analyze the performance data to identify which variations resonate best with your audience.

Continuous testing and refinement lead to more effective campaigns over time.

7. Budget Allocation Based on Performance: Gemini AI can help optimize your budget allocation by identifying high-performing channels and campaigns. Allocate more budget to channels that deliver a positive return on investment and adjust spending based on real-time performance metrics.

8. Ad Copy Optimization with Natural Language Processing: Utilize Gemini AI's natural language processing capabilities to optimize ad copy. Ensure that your messaging aligns with the language preferences of your target audience and resonates with their emotions. Well-crafted and linguistically optimized ad copy enhances engagement and conversion rates.

9. Retargeting Strategies: Implement retargeting campaigns using Gemini AI to re-engage users who have previously interacted with your brand. Analyze user behavior to determine the optimal timing and messaging for retargeting efforts, increasing the likelihood of conversions.

10. Data-Driven Decision-Making: Use Gemini AI to make data-driven decisions throughout the campaign lifecycle. Analyze real-time performance metrics, adjust strategies based on insights, and make informed decisions to optimize your advertising spend continuously.

By incorporating these strategies with the support of Gemini AI, you can create targeted digital marketing campaigns that not only optimize your advertising spend but also enhance the overall effectiveness of your marketing efforts.

Online Courses and Webinars

Leveraging Google Gemini AI for creating, structuring, and selling online courses and webinars involves tapping into the AI's capabilities in content creation, organization, and market analysis. Here's a step-by-step guide on how to utilize Gemini AI to build and monetize educational content effectively:

1. Identify Your Educational Niche: Use Gemini AI to analyze market trends and identify a niche for your online courses or webinars. Understand the demand for specific topics, target audience preferences, and potential competitors in the educational space.

2. Content Creation with Gemini AI:
Leverage Gemini AI's content creation capabilities to produce engaging and informative course materials. Generate course outlines, lesson plans, and even multimedia content using the AI's natural language processing and creative abilities.

3. Structuring Your Courses: Use Gemini AI to organize and structure your courses effectively. Develop clear modules, chapters, and learning objectives. Ensure that the content flows logically, providing a seamless learning experience for your audience.

4. Interactive Elements and Engagement: Incorporate interactive elements into your courses, such as quizzes, polls, and discussions. Gemini AI can assist in creating engaging interactive content that enhances the learning experience and keeps participants actively involved.

5. Personalization for Individual Learners: Utilize Gemini AI to personalize the learning experience for individual learners. The AI can analyze user data to understand learning preferences and recommend specific modules or content based on each learner's needs.

6. Automated Feedback and Assessments: Implement automated feedback systems using Gemini AI. The AI can evaluate assessments, provide instant feedback to learners, and adapt the difficulty level of the content based on individual performance.

7. Market Analysis for Pricing and Positioning: Leverage Gemini AI's market analysis capabilities to determine an optimal pricing strategy for your courses. Analyze competitor pricing, assess the perceived value of your content, and position your courses in a way that attracts your target audience.

8. Marketing and Promotions: Utilize Gemini AI for marketing and promotional activities. The AI can help identify the most effective channels for promoting your courses, craft compelling marketing copy, and optimize advertising strategies to reach a wider audience.

9. Sales Funnel Optimization: Implement a sales funnel for your online courses, from awareness to conversion. Use Gemini AI to optimize each stage of the funnel, ensuring that your marketing efforts are tailored to the needs and behaviors of potential learners.

10. Data-Driven Decision-Making: Continuously analyze data generated by Gemini AI to make informed decisions. Monitor learner engagement, assess course performance, and use insights to refine your courses, marketing strategies, and overall business approach.

11. Customer Support Automation: Implement automated customer support using Gemini AI. Address common queries, provide instant assistance, and enhance the overall user experience by integrating AI-driven support mechanisms.

12. Continuous Improvement: Use Gemini AI to gather feedback from learners and make continuous improvements to your courses. Analyze feedback data to identify areas for enhancement, ensuring that your educational offerings evolve with the needs of your audience.

By incorporating Gemini AI into the process of creating, structuring, and selling online courses and webinars, you can streamline your educational offerings, enhance learner engagement, and optimize the overall success of your online education business.

The potential for recurring income with minimal additional effort

In the realm of business, the pursuit of lasting success often leads entrepreneurs to the golden grail of sustainable revenue—recurring income. Picture a stream that flows continuously, requiring just a gentle push to keep it in motion. This is the essence of a revenue model that demands minimal additional effort, yet promises consistent returns.

Our journey into the potential for recurring income begins with a fundamental understanding of its allure. It's not merely about revenue; it's about the art of cultivating a self-sustaining ecosystem where income flows effortlessly.

Why is recurring income the heartbeat of prosperous businesses? Delve into the myriad advantages that unfold when entrepreneurs embrace models that prioritize consistency. From reducing the burden on day-to-day operations to creating a foundation for scalability, the benefits are as diverse as they are compelling.

Imagine a subscription model that operates like clockwork, demanding only initial setup and periodic tweaks. We explore the elegance of automated subscription services, where customers seamlessly contribute to the revenue stream without constant oversight. This is not just a business model;

it's a well-calibrated engine designed for enduring success.

In the quest for recurring income, creating a community isn't just a strategy; it's a mindset. Dive into the world of membership programs designed not just for revenue but for fostering genuine loyalty. Discover how engaged communities become advocates, contributing to a sustained income flow that requires minimal effort to maintain.

Anticipating the future is a powerful tool, especially when it comes to retaining subscribers. Uncover the potential of predictive analytics in identifying and addressing churn risks proactively. It's not just about keeping subscribers; it's about keeping the revenue flowing effortlessly.

Engagement shouldn't be forced; it should be inspired. Explore strategies that incentivize participation and loyalty. By creating a system where subscribers are naturally motivated to stay involved, the effort required for retention becomes almost negligible.

The beauty of an effective revenue model lies in its ability to grow organically. Delve into the art of cross-selling and upselling—strategies that seamlessly enhance the value offered to customers. Discover how supplementary offerings can be introduced with minimal disruption, creating a harmonious revenue ecosystem.

In the ever-evolving marketplace, adaptability is key. Explore the role of continuous monitoring and adjustment, ensuring that your recurring income model stays in sync with changing consumer trends. It's not just about reacting; it's about proactively aligning your offerings with the dynamic expectations of your audience.

As we conclude this exploration into the potential for recurring income with minimal additional effort, envision a business landscape where revenue flows effortlessly, and entrepreneurs thrive. The path to lasting success lies not in constant exertion but in the art of setting up systems that sustain themselves, allowing business owners to focus on innovation and growth.

Chapter 3:

Your Path to $1,000/Month

Niche Identification

In the vast landscape of entrepreneurship, selecting the right niche is not just a decision; it's a strategic move that sets the tone for success. This chapter unfolds the art of strategically choosing a niche, where personal passion converges seamlessly with the demands of the market.

Picture embarking on a journey where your genuine interests harmonize with the needs of the market. The chapter begins with the understanding that the road to a flourishing venture commences with a well-thought-out choice of niche. It's not merely about occupying a space but about embarking on a thoughtful journey that lays the foundation for sustained success.

The narrative begins with introspection—identifying and defining your authentic interests. What sparks your curiosity? What topics or activities resonate with your passion? This self-discovery becomes the cornerstone, the genuine starting point for any successful venture.

The story then shifts to the broader canvas of market demand. What are people actively seeking? What solutions, products, or services are in high demand? Understanding the pulse of the market becomes the guiding compass, ensuring your chosen niche not only aligns with your passion but also meets real needs.

The magic unfolds at the intersection—a sweet spot where your interests and market demand align seamlessly. Here, we delve into strategies for identifying niches that not only resonate with your passion but also fulfill genuine needs within the market. It's about discovering that sweet spot where success feels almost predestined.

Every niche comes with its set of challenges, including competition and market saturation. The narrative navigates the nuances of these factors, offering insights on identifying niches that provide growth opportunities while remaining mindful of potential obstacles.

Strategic decision-making relies on a robust foundation of information. Dive into the art of niche validation through meticulous research. What are the prevailing trends? Who are the key players? How can you position yourself uniquely within the chosen niche? We unravel the steps to validate your niche choice with unwavering confidence.

Selecting a niche is not merely a transient decision; it's a commitment to a journey. The chapter concludes by emphasizing the importance of aligning your niche selection with long-term goals. How does your chosen niche contribute to the overarching vision for your venture? We explore the strategic foresight needed to ensure sustained success.

As we conclude this exploration into strategically selecting a niche, envision a venture where your passion seamlessly intertwines with market demand. It's not just about finding a space; it's about creating a niche that becomes uniquely yours—a space where your journey aligns with the heartbeat of your audience, setting the stage for a performance that resonates and endures.

Attract a dedicated audience through a focused and optimized approach

In the bustling digital landscape, attracting a dedicated audience requires more than just visibility—it demands a focused and optimized approach. Let's explore the art of capturing the attention of a committed audience, navigating the intricacies of online presence, and optimizing strategies for a lasting impact.

Imagine your online presence as a canvas waiting for the strokes of your unique story. This chapter begins with the essence of crafting a digital presence that reflects your brand, values, and offerings. It's not just about being present; it's about leaving an indelible mark that resonates with your target audience.

The narrative then shifts to the heart of audience attraction—understanding who they are. We explore the strategies for creating detailed audience personas, unraveling the layers of their preferences, behaviors, and needs. By truly knowing your audience, you lay the groundwork for a connection that goes beyond mere visibility.

In the digital realm, content is the currency that buys attention. Dive into the art of creating compelling and valuable content that serves as a magnet, drawing your audience in. From engaging blog posts to captivating social media updates, we explore content strategies that resonate with your dedicated followers.

Visibility matters, and in the vast digital landscape, it's crucial to be easily discoverable. This section delves into the world of search engine optimization (SEO), offering insights on how to optimize your content for search engines. Discover the power of keywords, meta tags, and other

SEO techniques that enhance your online presence.

Attracting a dedicated audience is not a one-way street; it's about building a community. Explore the strategies for fostering engagement—responding to comments, hosting interactive sessions, and creating a space where your audience feels heard and valued. A community is not just an audience; it's a tribe that advocates for your brand.

Social media is a dynamic stage where your brand performs. Uncover the secrets of effective social media usage—from choosing the right platforms to creating shareable content. We navigate the nuances of social media marketing, offering tips on how to build a genuine following that extends beyond mere numbers.

In the digital noise, email remains a direct channel to your audience's inbox. Explore the art of email marketing as a relationship builder. We delve into strategies for crafting compelling newsletters, automated campaigns, and personalized communication that nurtures a connection with your dedicated audience.

The story concludes with a crucial chapter—analyzing and adapting. In the ever-evolving digital landscape, understanding analytics is paramount. Discover the tools and metrics that help you assess the effectiveness of your strategies. By analyzing data, you gain insights that guide your adaptive approach to audience attraction.

As we conclude this exploration into attracting a dedicated audience, envision a digital realm where your brand not only exists but flourishes. It's not just about attracting attention; it's about creating a magnetic force that keeps your dedicated audience coming back for more. The journey continues as you optimize, engage, and adapt, forging lasting connections in the ever-expanding digital universe.

Building Your Platform

In the expansive digital landscape, establishing a presence on platforms like a blog, YouTube channel, or e-commerce website requires more than just a digital storefront—it demands a strategic approach with a focus on SEO optimization for organic traffic. Let's delve into the intricacies of building and optimizing these platforms to attract a substantial and organic audience.

Imagine your online presence as a hub—a central space where your audience can gather. This chapter initiates with the process of crafting your blog, YouTube channel, or e-commerce website. We explore the key elements of design, user experience, and functionality, setting the stage for a digital space that not only captures attention but keeps visitors engaged.

The narrative then shifts to the pivotal decision of choosing the right platform. Whether it's a blog for written content, a YouTube channel for video engagement, or an e-commerce website for product offerings, each platform has its unique strengths. We guide you through the decision-making process, considering your content type, target audience, and business goals.

At the core of digital visibility lies the art of Search Engine Optimization (SEO). Dive into the foundations of SEO, exploring the significance of keyword research, meta tags, and content structure. Understand how a solid SEO foundation is the bedrock for organic visibility on search engines, ensuring that your digital hub is easily discoverable.

Content is the heartbeat of your digital hub. Explore strategies for creating content that resonates with your audience. From blog posts that address specific queries to YouTube videos that captivate, we unravel the nuances of content creation. Each piece is not just an addition but a strategic move to enhance organic reach.

User experience is paramount in retaining your audience. We explore the principles of user-friendly design and navigation, ensuring that visitors can seamlessly explore your digital hub. From intuitive layouts to clear calls-to-action, every element is strategically placed to enhance the overall user experience.

Whether it's incorporating images, infographics, or videos, multimedia is a powerful tool for engagement. Discover how to strategically integrate multimedia elements into your content, creating a dynamic and immersive experience for your audience. Each visual or auditory component contributes to both user engagement and SEO optimization.

For those venturing into e-commerce, optimization is a multifaceted endeavor. Explore strategies for optimizing product pages, streamlining the checkout process, and implementing e-commerce SEO best practices. A well-optimized e-commerce website not only attracts organic traffic but converts visitors into customers.

The story concludes with a chapter on performance analysis and iteration. Uncover the tools and metrics that help you gauge the effectiveness of your digital hub. By analyzing performance data, you gain insights into what works and what can be improved. This iterative approach ensures that your digital presence evolves with the changing dynamics of the digital landscape.

As we conclude this exploration into establishing a blog, YouTube channel, or e-commerce website with SEO optimization, envision a digital hub that not only exists but thrives. It's not just about creating a space; it's about cultivating a digital ecosystem where your audience discovers, engages, and returns organically. The journey continues as you refine, optimize, and adapt to the evolving landscape of digital visibility.

Ensure a user-friendly platform that engages and retains your audience

Creating a digital space that is both inviting and engaging is not merely about design; it's a strategic endeavor to ensure a user-friendly platform that captivates and retains your audience seamlessly.

Envision your online presence as more than just a platform—it's a welcoming haven where visitors feel a sense of belonging. This chapter begins with the understanding that user-friendliness is not just a feature; it's the essence that sets the stage for a lasting connection with your audience.

The journey starts with the significance of intuitive navigation. Explore strategies to design a platform where visitors can effortlessly navigate through content. Clear menus, well-organized categories, and a logical flow empower users to explore seamlessly, ensuring they find what they seek without unnecessary hurdles.

In a digital era dominated by mobile devices, the importance of responsiveness cannot be overstated. We delve into strategies to not just make your platform accessible but to optimize it for various devices. A responsive design ensures a consistent and engaging experience, regardless of whether users access your platform from a desktop, tablet, or smartphone.

Patience may be a virtue, but in the digital realm, it's a precious commodity. Uncover the secrets of optimizing your platform for swift page loading. From image optimization to leveraging browser caching, learn techniques that keep loading times minimal, preventing your audience from losing interest due to sluggish performance.

Engagement thrives on clear calls-to-action. This section explores the art of strategically placing buttons, links, and prompts that guide users toward desired actions. Whether it's making a purchase, subscribing, or navigating to another page, well-defined calls-to-action enhance user interaction and contribute to a seamless experience.

The journey continues with the importance of accessible and inclusive design. Learn how to create a platform that caters to users with diverse needs and abilities. Incorporating features like alt text for images and ensuring adequate color contrast contributes to a design that is universally accessible.

Engagement is not just about consumption; it's about interaction. Explore the incorporation of interactive elements that invite user participation. From quizzes to polls and comment sections, these features transform your platform into a dynamic space where users actively contribute to the conversation.

User feedback is a valuable asset for refinement. Discover strategies for incorporating feedback mechanisms into your platform. By actively seeking and implementing user input, you ensure that your platform evolves in ways that resonate with your audience, fostering a sense of involvement and ownership.

The story concludes with the concept of personalization—an approach that tailors the user experience. Explore strategies for implementing features that allow users to customize their interactions. From personalized recommendations to user-specific dashboards, personalization adds a layer of individualized engagement, making each visit feel uniquely tailored.

As we conclude this exploration into ensuring a user-friendly platform, visualize a digital haven where engagement is not just a feature but a fundamental quality. It's not merely about creating a space; it's about crafting an environment where users feel welcomed, engaged, and inclined to return. The journey persists as you refine, optimize, and adapt to meet the evolving expectations of your audience.

Leveraging Gemini AI for Success

Embark on a transformative journey as we explore the incredible capabilities of Gemini AI, designed by Google to revolutionize digital strategies. In this step-by-step guide, we'll navigate the seamless integration of Gemini AI into your processes, covering content creation, customer service automation, and data analysis.

1. Getting Started with Gemini AI

- Begin by creating your Gemini AI account. The registration process is user-friendly, allowing quick access to the platform's expansive features.

- Once inside, take a moment to familiarize yourself with the Gemini AI platform. Its intuitive layout caters to content creation, customer service, and data analysis needs.

2. Content Creation with Gemini AI

- Dive into the content creation capabilities of Gemini AI. Input your preferences—choose a topic, define the tone—and witness the platform generate high-quality, SEO-optimized content effortlessly.
- Enhance the visibility of your content through SEO optimization. Incorporate relevant keywords seamlessly, ensuring your content resonates with your target audience.

3. Customer Service Automation

- Elevate your customer service game by implementing Gemini AI chatbots. Train these bots to handle a spectrum of common queries, providing round-the-clock support for enhanced user experiences.

- Explore strategies to dynamically engage users through Gemini AI. Personalized responses and interactive elements contribute to a responsive and satisfying customer service experience.

4. Data Analysis with Gemini AI

- Utilize Gemini AI's robust data processing and interpretation capabilities. Input datasets and witness the platform unveil valuable trends and patterns, contributing to informed decision-making.

- Broaden your data analysis horizons by seamlessly integrating external data sources. Gemini AI effortlessly consolidates data from various channels for a more comprehensive analysis.

- Tailor your data reports to specific business needs. Create visualizations, charts, and comprehensive reports that align with your organizational objectives.

5. Continuous Learning and Optimization

- Stay abreast of Gemini AI's evolving features and capabilities to optimize your strategies continuously.

- Adopt an iterative approach. Regularly analyze performance, gather user feedback, and refine your strategies to maximize the benefits of Gemini AI.

As you follow this guide, seamlessly integrating Gemini AI into your digital toolkit, you'll unlock new possibilities in automation, efficiency, and strategic decision-making.

Optimize your strategies for consistent growth and income

In the dynamic landscape of AI-driven passive income, optimizing your strategies is pivotal for achieving consistent growth and a steady income stream. Let's explore how you can fine-tune your approach using Gemini AI.

Analyze Performance Metrics: Leverage Gemini AI's analytics capabilities to delve into performance metrics. Examine content engagement, customer service interactions, and data analysis results. Identify patterns and insights that can guide your optimization efforts.

Content Refinement: Continuously refine your content creation strategy with Gemini AI. Analyze audience feedback, track performance metrics, and adapt your content based on what resonates most with your target audience. Ensure a balance between relevance, quality, and SEO optimization.

Customer Service Iterations: Iterate on your customer service strategies by analyzing chatbot interactions and user feedback. Identify common pain points and enhance chatbot responses. Tailor your customer engagement strategies based on evolving user needs.

Data-Driven Decision Making: Utilize Gemini AI's data analysis capabilities for informed decision-making. Regularly review and update your data analysis methodologies. Adjust your data integration sources to stay aligned with evolving business requirements.

Explore Additional Monetization Avenues: Diversify your income streams by exploring additional monetization avenues with Gemini AI. Consider new partnerships, affiliate programs, or innovative content formats. Gemini AI's versatility allows you to adapt and explore various income-generating possibilities.

Audience Engagement Strategies: Develop strategies to enhance audience engagement. Use Gemini AI insights to understand your audience better. Tailor your content and engagement initiatives to build a loyal and active community around your niche.

Optimization Through Automation: Automate repetitive tasks using Gemini AI to optimize time and resources. Whether it's automating content creation processes or refining customer service workflows, find opportunities to enhance efficiency through automation.

Stay Informed and Adaptive: Regularly update your knowledge on Gemini AI's evolving features. Stay informed about industry trends, algorithm changes, and emerging opportunities. An adaptive approach ensures that you are always ahead of the curve.

By continually optimizing your strategies with Gemini AI, you'll create a robust foundation for consistent growth and income. Remember, the key lies in adaptability, data-driven decision-making, and a commitment to refining your approach based on real-time insights.

Monetization Mastery

In the ever-evolving landscape of AI-powered passive income, unlocking diverse monetization avenues is key to financial success. With the capabilities of Gemini AI, you have a versatile tool to explore and implement various strategies.

Let's delve into some effective monetization approaches:

Affiliate Marketing Mastery: Harness the power of Gemini AI to create engaging content enriched with affiliate links. Seamlessly integrate these links within AI-generated articles, blog posts, or social media content. When your audience clicks and makes purchases through these links, you earn passive commissions.

Ads for Incremental Revenue: Leverage Gemini AI to optimize your platform for ads. Whether on a blog, website, or social media channel, use AI-generated content to attract a larger audience. As your traffic grows, strategically incorporate ad spaces using platforms like Google AdSense to maximize your ad revenue.

Sponsored Content Collaboration: Partner with brands to create sponsored content that resonates with your audience. Gemini AI can assist in crafting compelling narratives, ensuring sponsored posts seamlessly integrate into your content strategy. Build collaborations that align with your niche, enhancing both your brand and the sponsor's visibility.

Digital Product Sales Revolution: Utilize Gemini AI's content creation prowess to develop and market digital products. Whether it's e-books, online courses, or exclusive webinars, craft valuable digital offerings. Sell these products directly to your audience, creating a channel for recurring income with minimal additional effort.

By integrating these monetization strategies, you can optimize your income streams and diversify revenue sources. Gemini AI acts as your ally in content creation, ensuring your approach is not only strategic but also adaptive to the ever-changing digital landscape. Explore, experiment, and let Gemini AI be the catalyst for your financial success.

Craft a balanced approach that maximizes your revenue potential

In the realm of AI-driven passive income, achieving financial success requires a balanced approach that maximizes your revenue potential. With Gemini AI as your strategic ally, consider the following principles for crafting a well-rounded and effective strategy:

Diversification for Resilience: Diversify your income streams to build resilience. Embrace a mix of affiliate marketing, ad revenue, sponsored content, and digital product sales. This diversified approach ensures that you're not overly reliant on a single source, mitigating risks and enhancing financial stability.

Strategic Affiliate Integration: Seamlessly integrate affiliate marketing into your content strategy. Use Gemini AI to create engaging and informative content that naturally incorporates affiliate links. Strive for authenticity, ensuring that the products or services you promote align with your audience's interests and needs.

Optimized Ad Spaces: Strategically optimize your platform for ads using Gemini AI-generated content. Balance the placement and frequency of ads to maximize revenue without compromising user experience. Leverage AI insights to understand user behavior and tailor ad placements accordingly.

Engaging Sponsored Collaborations: Cultivate meaningful partnerships with brands for sponsored content. Use Gemini AI to craft compelling narratives that resonate with your audience while seamlessly integrating the sponsor's message. Prioritize collaborations that align with your niche, fostering authenticity and trust.

Curated Digital Offerings: Leverage Gemini AI's content creation capabilities to curate and market digital products. Craft e-books, online courses, or webinars that provide genuine value to your audience.

Optimize pricing and promotional strategies to encourage sales and unlock a channel for recurring income.

Data-Driven Decision Making: Utilize Gemini AI for data analysis to make informed decisions. Analyze the performance of each monetization strategy, identifying strengths and areas for improvement. Data-driven insights empower you to optimize your approach continuously.

Adaptability and Continuous Optimization: Stay adaptive in response to industry trends and user behavior. Regularly optimize your strategies based on Gemini AI analytics. Embrace a mindset of continuous improvement, refining your approach to align with evolving market dynamics.

By embracing this balanced approach, you'll create a resilient and dynamic revenue model with Gemini AI at its core. Continuously refine your strategies, experiment with new opportunities, and let the adaptability of Gemini AI guide you towards sustained financial success.

Scaling Your Efforts

In the dynamic landscape of AI-powered passive income, regularly analyzing performance metrics is crucial for refining strategies and optimizing outcomes. With Gemini AI's robust analytics capabilities, you can gain valuable insights into the effectiveness of your initiatives. Here's a guide on how to make the most of Gemini AI's analytics:

Accessing Analytics Dashboard: Navigate to Gemini AI's analytics dashboard to gain a comprehensive overview of your performance metrics. Familiarize yourself with the various metrics available, including content engagement, customer interactions, and data analysis results.

Content Engagement Analysis: Dive into content engagement metrics to understand how your audience interacts with AI-generated content. Analyze factors such as click-through rates, time spent on pages, and social shares. Identify high-performing content and patterns that resonate with your audience.

Customer Service Interaction Metrics: Explore the analytics related to customer service interactions facilitated by Gemini AI chatbots. Evaluate response times, user satisfaction ratings, and common queries. Use this data to refine chatbot responses and enhance the overall user experience.

Data Analysis Effectiveness: Assess the effectiveness of data analysis initiatives by reviewing key metrics. Look at the accuracy of predictions, the depth of insights gained, and the relevance of data-driven decisions. Identify areas where data analysis can be fine-tuned for more impactful results.

Conversion Tracking: Implement conversion tracking mechanisms within the analytics dashboard. Monitor the conversion rates of affiliate links, ad clicks, and digital product sales. Understand the factors influencing user conversions and optimize your strategies accordingly.

User Behavior Insights: Leverage Gemini AI's ability to provide insights into user behavior. Understand how your audience navigates your platform, their preferences, and the content types that resonate most. Use these insights to tailor your content and offerings to better meet user expectations.

Iterative Strategy Refinement: Adopt an iterative approach to strategy refinement based on analytics. Regularly review performance metrics and implement adjustments to content, marketing, and customer service strategies. Embrace a culture of continuous improvement to stay ahead of the curve.

Data-Driven Decision-Making: Emphasize data-driven decision-making in your overall strategy. Use Gemini AI analytics to inform high-stakes decisions, such as partnerships, content focus, and monetization strategies. Align your actions with real-time data to maximize impact.

By consistently delving into Gemini AI's analytics, you'll gain actionable insights that empower you to refine your approach, enhance user experiences, and optimize your passive income strategies. Regular analysis is the cornerstone of success in the ever-evolving landscape of AI-driven income generation.

<u>Optimize your strategies based on insights and scale up your efforts for increased income</u>

In the dynamic world of AI-powered passive income, the journey doesn't end with insightful analysis; it extends to strategic optimization and scaling. With Gemini AI as your ally, follow these steps to fine-tune your strategies and scale up your efforts for increased income:

Identify Performance Insights: Begin by extracting actionable insights from Gemini AI's analytics. Identify patterns, trends, and areas of success or improvement across content engagement, customer service interactions, and data analysis. Pinpoint key performance indicators that align with your income goals.

Content Refinement for Impact: Refine your content creation strategy based on performance insights. Emphasize the creation of content that resonates most with your audience. Adjust tone, style, and topics to align with what garners the highest engagement. Use Gemini AI to iteratively generate content that meets evolving preferences.

Adapt Monetization Strategies: Fine-tune your monetization strategies in response to analytics. If certain avenues are consistently outperforming others, allocate resources accordingly. Optimize ad placements, explore new affiliate partnerships, and adjust pricing strategies for digital products based on conversion rates.

Enhance Customer Service Dynamics: Elevate your customer service game by incorporating insights from chatbot interactions. Identify common user queries and refine chatbot responses. Implement interactive elements based on user feedback to enhance overall satisfaction. A well-tailored customer service experience contributes to user retention and loyalty.

Data-Driven Marketing Campaigns: Leverage data-driven insights to optimize your digital marketing efforts. Craft targeted campaigns informed by user behavior, preferences, and market trends identified through Gemini AI. Allocate your advertising spend strategically, focusing on channels and strategies that yield the highest returns.

Explore New Niches and Ventures: Consider expanding into new niches or ventures based on analytics. If there's a clear demand or interest in specific topics or products, explore opportunities to diversify your content and offerings. Gemini AI can assist in generating ideas and insights for potential expansion.

Invest in Automation for Efficiency: Utilize Gemini AI's automation capabilities to streamline repetitive tasks. Automate content scheduling, social media posts, and basic customer service inquiries. Freeing up time through automation allows you to focus on strategic aspects that contribute to income growth.

Monitor Scalability Challenges: As you scale up efforts, be mindful of potential scalability challenges. Ensure that your infrastructure, whether in terms of hosting, customer service capabilities, or content management, can seamlessly accommodate increased demands. Gemini AI's scalability can be an asset in this regard.

By optimizing your strategies based on Gemini AI insights and scaling up your efforts strategically, you'll create a roadmap for sustained income growth. This iterative process ensures that your passive income endeavors remain dynamic, adaptive, and aligned with the evolving landscape of AI-driven opportunities.

Chapter 4:
Overcoming Challenges and Ethical Considerations

Ensuring Content Authenticity

As you embark on your AI-powered passive income journey with Gemini AI, the challenge of maintaining authenticity in AI-generated content becomes a crucial consideration. Here's a comprehensive guide on navigating this challenge and ensuring that your content remains genuine and valuable:

Set Clear Guidelines: Establish clear guidelines for AI-generated content. Clearly define the tone, style, and values that align with your brand or personal voice. Provide specific instructions to Gemini AI to ensure content output meets your authenticity standards.

Human Touch in Editing: Introduce a human touch in the editing process. While Gemini AI excels at content creation, human editors can refine and personalize the content to add that crucial authentic touch. Edit for voice consistency, relevance, and cultural nuances.

Regular Quality Checks: Implement a system of regular quality checks for AI-generated content. Develop a checklist that includes authenticity markers such as factual accuracy, coherence, and relevance to your niche. Regular reviews help maintain the overall quality of your content.

Incorporate Personal Insights: Infuse your personal insights into the content. While Gemini AI is a powerful tool, your unique perspective, experiences, and expertise can elevate the authenticity of the content. Share anecdotes, personal reflections, and real-world examples to connect with your audience.

Blend AI with Original Content: Strike a balance by blending AI-generated content with original pieces. Craft certain articles, posts, or sections without AI assistance to ensure a direct expression of your voice. This combination adds a layer of authenticity that resonates with your audience.

Engage in Dialogue with Your Audience: Foster an open dialogue with your audience. Encourage feedback and actively respond to comments. Addressing audience inquiries and participating in discussions not only builds authenticity but also establishes a genuine connection with your community.

Disclose AI Involvement: Be transparent about the use of AI in content creation. Disclose to your audience that certain pieces are generated with the assistance of Gemini AI. Transparency builds trust and ensures that your audience appreciates the role of AI in your creative process.

Prioritize Value and Relevance: Emphasize value and relevance in your content. Whether AI-generated or not, content that genuinely helps or entertains your audience is more likely to be perceived as authentic. Prioritize substance over sheer volume, aligning with your audience's needs.

Cultivate a Consistent Brand Voice: Cultivate a consistent brand voice that permeates all content, AI-generated or otherwise. This consistency establishes a recognizable identity, making it easier for your audience to connect with and trust your content.

By implementing these strategies, you can successfully navigate the authenticity challenge associated with AI-generated content. Remember that authenticity is not compromised by using AI; it's enhanced when coupled with thoughtful curation, personalization, and a commitment to delivering meaningful value to your audience.

Tips for ensuring your content adds real value to your audience

Creating content that genuinely adds value to your audience is paramount for sustained success in the realm of AI-powered passive income. Here are tips to ensure your content resonates, informs, and provides real value:

Understand Your Audience: Conduct thorough audience research to understand the needs, preferences, and pain points of your target audience. Gemini AI can assist in analyzing trends and behaviors, helping you tailor content that directly addresses their concerns.

Solve Real Problems: Prioritize content that solves real problems or challenges your audience faces. Whether through tutorials, guides, or informative articles, aim to be a valuable resource. Use Gemini AI to generate content that directly addresses common queries within your niche.

Educate and Inform: Position yourself as an educational hub within your niche. Use Gemini AI to create content that informs and educates your audience on relevant topics. Providing valuable insights establishes your authority and fosters trust.

Consistent Quality over Quantity: Emphasize the quality of your content over sheer quantity. Gemini AI can assist in generating high-quality content, but it's essential to prioritize relevance, accuracy, and engagement. Regularly review and refine your content to maintain a high standard.

Engage in Dialogue: Foster a two-way communication channel with your audience. Encourage comments, questions, and discussions. Use Gemini AI to analyze audience interactions and tailor your content to address their interests and concerns.

Keep Up with Trends: Utilize Gemini AI's capabilities to stay informed about emerging trends in your niche. Create content that reflects current trends and developments, ensuring that your audience receives the most up-to-date and relevant information.

Diversify Content Formats: Explore various content formats to cater to different preferences. Gemini AI can assist in generating not only written content but also visual and interactive elements. Incorporate videos, infographics, and interactive posts to enhance engagement.

Provide Actionable Insights: Ensure that your content offers actionable insights. Whether it's step-by-step guides, practical tips, or actionable takeaways, Gemini AI can assist in creating content that empowers your audience to implement what they learn.

Evoke Emotion: Craft content that evokes emotion and resonates with your audience on a personal level. Use Gemini AI to infuse storytelling elements that connect with readers emotionally, making your content more memorable and impactful.

Regularly Assess Audience Feedback: Actively seek and analyze audience feedback. Use Gemini AI to process and understand the sentiments expressed by your audience. Adjust your content strategy based on constructive feedback to continually enhance value.

By integrating these tips into your content creation strategy, you'll not only maximize the potential of Gemini AI but also create a valuable and engaging experience for your audience. Consistently delivering real value establishes trust, fosters audience loyalty, and positions you as a reliable source within your niche.

Ethical AI Use

In the ever-evolving landscape of AI-powered passive income, maintaining ethical practices and compliance with digital marketing standards is essential. Here are guidelines to help you navigate the ethical considerations associated with AI and digital marketing:

Adhere to Data Privacy Regulations: Prioritize the privacy of user data. Familiarize yourself with and comply with data protection regulations such as GDPR

(General Data Protection Regulation) or other applicable laws in your region. Ensure transparency in how user data is collected, used, and stored.

Transparent AI Usage Disclosure: Clearly disclose the use of AI in your content creation and marketing processes. Inform your audience about the assistance provided by Gemini AI in generating content. Transparency builds trust and helps your audience understand the technology behind your offerings.

Avoid Misleading Claims: Steer clear of exaggerated or misleading claims in your content. Whether promoting products, services, or the capabilities of AI, provide accurate and transparent information.

Gemini AI-generated content should align with ethical marketing principles, emphasizing authenticity.

Respect User Consent: Obtain explicit consent for data collection and marketing communications. Clearly communicate the purposes for which user data will be used and seek permission before implementing any tracking or marketing strategies. Gemini AI can assist in crafting transparent and user-friendly consent forms.

Fair and Unbiased Content Creation: Mitigate biases in AI-generated content. Regularly review and fine-tune the training data used by Gemini AI to minimize biases. Strive for fair representation in content creation, ensuring that diverse perspectives are considered.

Ethical Affiliate Marketing: When engaging in affiliate marketing, select products or services that align with ethical standards. Avoid promoting products with questionable reputations or that may compromise the trust of your audience. Gemini AI can assist in creating content that promotes ethical affiliate partnerships.

Non-Discriminatory Advertising: Ensure that your advertising efforts do not discriminate against any individual or group. Review ad targeting parameters to prevent unintentional biases. Gemini AI can assist in crafting inclusive and non-discriminatory content.

AI Content Review: Regularly review AI-generated content to ensure it aligns with ethical standards. Implement a process for content review that includes checking for accuracy, relevance, and adherence to ethical guidelines. Human oversight is crucial in maintaining ethical content.

Stay Informed on AI Ethics: Stay abreast of developments in AI ethics. Regularly update your knowledge on ethical considerations in AI, digital marketing, and content creation. Attend industry conferences, participate in forums, and engage with AI ethics resources to remain well-informed.

Community Engagement and Feedback: Encourage community engagement and feedback regarding your AI-powered content. Foster a community where users feel comfortable expressing concerns or providing insights. Use this feedback loop to refine your practices and address ethical considerations.

By integrating these guidelines into your AI-powered passive income strategies, you'll demonstrate a commitment to ethical standards, build trust with your audience, and contribute to the responsible use of AI in digital marketing.

Uphold ethical practices in your AI-powered ventures

As you navigate the landscape of AI-powered passive income, maintaining ethical practices is paramount for long-term success and positive impact. Here's a guide on upholding ethical standards in your AI-powered ventures, especially with the assistance of Gemini AI:

Prioritize Transparency: Transparency is key to ethical AI usage. Clearly communicate to your audience that AI, specifically Gemini AI, is involved in content creation and other processes. This transparency fosters trust and ensures your audience is aware of the technology behind your ventures.

User Empowerment and Informed Consent: Empower users by providing them with clear and accessible information about how AI is used. Seek informed consent for data collection, content personalization, and other AI-driven activities. Users should have the ability to opt in or out based on their preferences.

Bias Mitigation: Actively work to mitigate biases in AI-generated content. Regularly review and refine the training data used by Gemini AI to ensure fair representation. Aim for content that is inclusive, unbiased, and respects diverse perspectives.

Accountability and Oversight: Establish accountability mechanisms for AI-generated content. Implement human oversight to review and monitor the output of Gemini AI. This oversight ensures that the content aligns with ethical standards, accuracy, and relevance.

Privacy Protection: Safeguard user privacy by adhering to data protection regulations. Familiarize yourself with applicable laws, such as GDPR, and implement measures to protect user data. Gemini AI can assist in crafting privacy-friendly content and interactions.

Fair Affiliate Marketing: Practice fairness in affiliate marketing endeavors. Choose affiliate partnerships based on ethical considerations, avoiding products or services that may harm your audience.

Disclose affiliate relationships transparently to maintain trust.

Non-Discriminatory Practices: Commit to non-discriminatory practices in content creation and marketing. Review targeting parameters to prevent unintentional biases. Ensure that your AI-powered ventures promote inclusivity and do not perpetuate stereotypes.

Continuous Learning and Adaptation: Stay informed about ethical considerations in AI and digital marketing. Engage in continuous learning, attend industry events, and adapt your practices based on emerging ethical standards. Gemini AI's evolving features may also come with new ethical considerations, so staying updated is crucial.

Community Engagement and Feedback: Foster an open dialogue with your community. Encourage feedback on your AI-powered ventures and actively address concerns. Engaging with your audience helps build a community that values ethical practices and transparency.

Advocate for Ethical AI Use: Be an advocate for ethical AI use within your industry. Share insights, best practices, and contribute to discussions on responsible AI. By actively participating in ethical considerations, you contribute to a positive and responsible AI ecosystem.

By incorporating these ethical guidelines into your AI-powered ventures, you not only adhere to responsible practices but also contribute to the overall positive perception of AI in digital endeavors. Upholding ethical standards ensures the longevity and positive impact of your AI-powered passive income initiatives.

Addressing Market Saturation

In the competitive landscape of AI-powered passive income, where more individuals are harnessing the potential of platforms like Google Gemini AI, standing out is crucial. Here's a comprehensive guide to help you differentiate your content and offerings, ensuring you carve a niche and captivate your audience:

Define Your Unique Value Proposition (UVP): Clearly articulate what sets your content and offerings apart. Identify your Unique Value Proposition (UVP) – the distinct value, benefits, or solutions that you provide. Your UVP should resonate with your target audience's needs and aspirations.

Specialize in a Niche: Instead of trying to appeal to a broad audience, specialize in a niche that aligns with your expertise and interests. Use Gemini AI to identify trending niches and create content that caters specifically to the unique needs of that niche.

Elevate Content Quality: Prioritize quality over quantity in your content creation. Use Gemini AI to produce high-quality, well-researched, and engaging content. A focus on excellence can make your offerings stand out in a sea of content.

Innovate with Content Formats: Experiment with diverse content formats. Gemini AI can assist in generating not only written content but also visual elements, videos, and interactive content. Innovate with formats that resonate with your audience, keeping them engaged and coming back for more.

Build a Distinct Brand Voice: Develop a unique and recognizable brand voice. Whether it's a conversational tone, a touch of humor, or a professional demeanor, ensure consistency across all your content. Gemini AI can adapt to your chosen brand voice, adding a cohesive element to your offerings.

Tell Compelling Stories: Humanize your content by telling compelling stories. Share personal anecdotes, case studies, or success stories related to your niche. Gemini AI can help in crafting narratives that resonate emotionally with your audience.

Offer Exclusive Insights: Provide exclusive insights and information that can't be easily found elsewhere. Leverage Gemini AI to analyze data and uncover unique trends or perspectives. Being a source of exclusive insights establishes you as an authority in your field.

Engage in Thought Leadership: Position yourself as a thought leader in your niche. Use Gemini AI to stay informed about the latest developments and share your informed opinions. Thought leadership builds credibility and attracts an audience seeking expert perspectives.

Interact and Respond: Actively engage with your audience through comments, social media, or forums. Respond to queries, feedback, and participate in discussions. Gemini AI can assist in crafting responses that maintain your brand voice and enhance user engagement.

Offer Value Beyond Content: Go beyond content creation. Offer additional value through webinars, workshops, or exclusive resources. Gemini AI can assist in generating materials for these additional offerings, creating a comprehensive and valuable experience for your audience.

Consistent Branding Across Platforms: Ensure consistent branding across all platforms. From your website to social media channels, maintain a cohesive brand image. Gemini AI can help in generating content that aligns seamlessly with your branding.

By implementing these strategies, you'll effectively differentiate your content and offerings in a potentially saturated market.

Utilize the capabilities of Gemini AI to enhance your creative processes, ensuring that your unique voice and value shine through in every piece of content you deliver.

Strategies for carving your unique space in the AI-powered passive income landscape

In the dynamic realm of AI-powered passive income, standing out is essential for sustained success. Here are effective strategies to carve your unique space in this landscape, leveraging the capabilities of Google Gemini AI:

Define Your Niche: Identify a niche that aligns with your expertise, interests, and market demand. Gemini AI can assist in analyzing trends to pinpoint a niche where you can offer unique value.

Craft a Compelling Brand Story: Develop a brand story that resonates with your audience. Utilize Gemini AI to weave a narrative that reflects your journey, values, and the unique proposition you bring to the AI-powered passive income space.

Innovate with Content Formats: Experiment with diverse content formats to keep your audience engaged. Gemini AI can generate not only written content but also visual elements, videos, and interactive content. Innovate with formats that set you apart.

Personalize User Experiences: Leverage Gemini AI's capabilities for personalized user experiences. Tailor your content and interactions based on user preferences and behaviors. Personalization enhances engagement and fosters a sense of connection.

Stay Ahead of Trends: Use Gemini AI to stay informed about emerging trends in your niche and the broader AI landscape. Being an early adopter of new technologies and trends positions you as an industry leader.

Collaborate and Network: Collaborate with others in the AI community. Gemini AI can help you identify potential collaborators or influencers. Networking expands your reach and brings fresh perspectives to your content.

Demonstrate Thought Leadership: Position yourself as a thought leader by consistently sharing insightful content. Use Gemini AI to analyze data and offer unique perspectives on industry developments. Thought leadership builds trust and credibility.

Create Exclusive Content: Offer exclusive content that sets you apart. Gemini AI can assist in generating in-depth analyses, reports, or insider insights. Exclusive content attracts and retains a dedicated audience.

Engage in Conversations: Actively engage with your audience through comments, social media, and forums. Use Gemini AI to respond to queries or comments in a way that reflects your brand voice and fosters a sense of community.

Optimize User Experience: Ensure a seamless user experience across all touchpoints. Gemini AI can help optimize content for user satisfaction. A positive user experience contributes to brand loyalty and attracts repeat visitors.

Offer Value Beyond Content: Go beyond traditional content creation. Host webinars, workshops, or provide downloadable resources. Gemini AI can contribute to the creation of materials for these additional offerings, enriching the value you provide.

Consistent Branding Across Platforms: Maintain a consistent brand image across all platforms. From your website to social media, use Gemini AI to generate content that aligns seamlessly with your branding strategy.

Embrace Continuous Learning: Stay abreast of industry developments and AI advancements. Gemini AI can assist in processing large volumes of information. Continuous learning ensures that you remain at the forefront of your niche.

By strategically implementing these strategies, you can carve your unique space in the AI-powered passive income landscape. Embrace the capabilities of Gemini AI to enhance your creativity, engage your audience, and establish a distinct presence in the ever-evolving world of AI-driven ventures.

Chapter 5:

Exploring Additional Income Streams

Code Generation

Embark on a journey into the realm of cutting-edge passive income as we delve into the lucrative world of selling code snippets and scripts crafted by the powerful Google Gemini AI. This chapter unveils a unique opportunity for tech enthusiasts, developers, and businesses to tap into the ingenuity of AI and transform it into a sustainable income stream.

Google Gemini AI stands as a beacon of innovation, and its prowess extends beyond traditional applications. In this section, we'll explore how Gemini AI's advanced capabilities in natural language processing and machine learning converge to create functional and efficient code snippets.

Understanding the pulse of the market is crucial. Discover how Gemini AI can assist in analyzing market trends and identifying the specific coding needs of developers and businesses. This insight ensures that the code snippets you offer align with the demands of the industry.

Dive into the process of building a diverse and marketable portfolio of code snippets. Gemini AI becomes your collaborator in crafting solutions that cater to different niches, enhancing your offerings and expanding your reach in the tech community.

Crafting a user-friendly platform to showcase your AI-generated code is paramount. Learn how Gemini AI can assist in creating engaging product descriptions, documentation, and even visually appealing representations of your code snippets, making them irresistible to potential buyers.

Determining the right pricing strategy is an art. Discover how to leverage Gemini AI's analytical capabilities to set competitive prices that reflect the value of your code snippets. This strategic approach ensures that your offerings are not only in demand but also financially rewarding.

In this section, we explore the dynamic landscape of digital marketing for code snippets. Gemini AI becomes a key ally in crafting compelling marketing content, optimizing ad campaigns, and effectively reaching your target audience of developers and businesses.

Establishing trust is paramount in the tech community. Learn how to implement a robust support system for your customers, and discover how Gemini AI can assist in generating documentation and responses that enhance the overall customer experience. Additionally, explore the benefits of automated updates to keep your code snippets current and relevant.

Scaling Your Code Business with Gemini AI
As your code business gains momentum, scalability becomes a focal point. Explore strategies for scaling your offerings, analyzing user feedback with Gemini AI, and identifying opportunities to expand

your product line, ensuring sustained growth in the competitive coding landscape.

This chapter is not just a guide; it's an invitation to revolutionize your passive income journey. Join us as we unlock the potential of Google Gemini AI in the world of coding, providing you with the tools and insights to create, market, and profit from AI-generated code snippets. Welcome to the future of tech-powered passive income.

Unlock the potential of a unique income stream catering to tech enthusiasts

In the dynamic world of passive income, an unparalleled opportunity awaits those who venture into the intersection of technology and innovation. This section unveils the gateway to a distinctive income stream tailored specifically for tech enthusiasts – the realm where Google Gemini AI transforms code generation into an art form.

Tech enthusiasts, ever-eager to explore the latest technological marvels, now have a new frontier to discover. With Google Gemini AI at the helm, the creation of code snippets becomes a fusion of creative artistry and functional precision. Each line of code becomes a masterpiece, resonating with the discerning tastes of tech aficionados.

Just as the tech community is diverse, so should be your offerings. Gemini AI empowers you to craft solutions that cater to a spectrum of tech interests – from app development to data science. The versatility of AI-generated code ensures that there's something for every tech palate, captivating a broad and passionate audience.

Captivating tech enthusiasts requires more than just functional code; it demands a showcase of brilliance. Discover how Gemini AI contributes to the creation of visually appealing product descriptions, engaging representations, and documentation that highlights the marvels of AI-generated code. Your offerings become not just tools but coveted works of technological art.

In the world of tech, where creativity meets functionality, pricing becomes an art. Explore the strategic approach of setting prices that reflect the unique blend of

Gemini AI's creativity and the practicality of the code snippets. The analytical capabilities of Gemini AI assist in determining a value that resonates with tech enthusiasts who appreciate the innovative essence of your offerings.

Marketing to tech enthusiasts is a nuanced dance. Uncover how Gemini AI becomes a strategic ally in crafting content that speaks the language of tech, optimizing ad campaigns, and effectively reaching your target audience. Position your AI-generated code as an indispensable tool for every tech aficionado, sparking their curiosity and aligning with their technological aspirations.

Tech enthusiasts thrive in communities that celebrate innovation. Dive into strategies for building a community around your AI-generated code. Gemini AI becomes the bridge that connects you with tech innovators, creating a space where ideas flow, feedback is exchanged, and your offerings become an integral part of the ongoing tech conversation.

As your tech-focused income stream gains momentum, scalability becomes a focal point. Discover how to scale your offerings with Gemini AI, analyzing user feedback, identifying emerging tech trends, and expanding your product line to stay at the forefront of the ever-evolving tech landscape.

Creative Writing Ventures:

In the vast expanse of the digital landscape, a unique opportunity awaits those who wish to weave their creativity into a lucrative income stream. This segment delves into the realm where Google Gemini AI becomes the muse, empowering individuals to showcase their artistic endeavors—be it poems, scripts, musical compositions, or other creative content—for sale in the boundless online marketplace.

With Google Gemini AI as your creative collaborator, the possibilities are as limitless as your imagination. Explore the synergy between human creativity and the augmenting power of AI as you embark on a journey to craft captivating pieces of art.

The canvas is yours, and Gemini AI stands ready to breathe life into your artistic visions.

For those who find solace in words and rhythm, Gemini AI becomes the poet's assistant. Dive into the art of crafting poems that resonate with emotions and evoke a connection with readers. Gemini AI's unique ability to understand nuances ensures that each verse is imbued with the essence of your emotions and the sophistication of AI-augmented expression.

For storytellers weaving tales of wonder, Gemini AI lends its creative flair to scriptwriting. Whether it's for film, television, or the digital realm, discover how Gemini AI assists in constructing narratives that captivate audiences. The result is not just a script but a compelling story brought to life by the collaboration of human imagination and AI ingenuity.

Music, the universal language, finds a new dimension with Gemini AI. Explore the art of musical composition, where your creativity harmonizes seamlessly with the augmenting capabilities of AI. Gemini AI aids in creating melodies that resonate, rhythms that captivate, and compositions that stand as a testament to the collaborative brilliance of human and artificial creativity.

Beyond poems, scripts, and musical compositions, Gemini AI opens doors to a diverse range of creative content. From digital art to innovative storytelling formats, discover how your creative palette can expand to cater to a broad audience hungry for unique and imaginative expressions. Gemini AI becomes the brushstroke that adds finesse to your artistic offerings.

Venturing into the online marketplace requires a carefully curated showcase. Learn how Gemini AI can assist in creating engaging product descriptions, visually appealing representations, and an online presence that resonates with potential buyers. Your artistic creations become not just commodities but coveted pieces of digital art, ready to be embraced by a global audience.

As you infuse your creativity with the augmenting power of Gemini AI, explore strategies for selling your artistic creations online. Whether it's through dedicated platforms, digital marketplaces, or your independent website, Gemini AI becomes your partner in navigating the online realm, ensuring that your creativity reaches those who appreciate and value your unique expressions.

Unleashing the artistic side of Gemini AI for additional income streams

In the ever-evolving landscape of passive income, a new frontier emerges where technology meets artistry. This section unveils the artistic side of Google Gemini AI, transforming it into a powerful ally for individuals seeking additional income streams through creative endeavors. Prepare to unleash the full spectrum of artistic possibilities and redefine the boundaries of passive income.

Discover how Gemini AI becomes a catalyst for the fusion of art and technology. As your creative partner, Gemini AI empowers you to explore a myriad of artistic expressions—from visual arts to literary masterpieces—infusing each creation with a touch of technological brilliance. This synthesis opens doors to untapped income streams that resonate with the intersection of creativity and innovation.

For visual artists, Gemini AI becomes the brushstroke that transforms the canvas of possibilities. Dive into the realm of digital art and design, where AI augments your creative process, offering suggestions, enhancing details, and bringing forth a new dimension to your artistic vision. Explore how these AI-infused creations become not only expressions of your talent but also sought-after pieces in the digital art marketplace.

Writers, poets, and storytellers, prepare to embark on a collaborative journey with Gemini AI. Witness how the language model enhances your writing process, suggesting creative twists, refining language, and contributing to the development of literary masterpieces. The result is not just words on a page but a fusion of human imagination and AI ingenuity, ready to be shared and monetized.

Musicians and composers, embrace the symphony of collaboration with Gemini AI. Explore how AI can assist in music composition, suggesting harmonies, refining melodies, and contributing to the creation of unique musical pieces. Unleash the artistic potential of Gemini AI in the realm of music, where every note becomes a testament to the collaborative brilliance of human and artificial creativity.

Gemini AI's artistic capabilities extend beyond traditional forms. Discover how it can assist in creating innovative storytelling formats—interactive narratives, immersive experiences, and unique content structures.

Gemini AI becomes the co-creator in pushing the boundaries of creativity, offering new and engaging ways to captivate audiences and generate income.

Transforming artistic expression into income requires a carefully crafted digital showcase. Learn how Gemini AI can contribute to creating visually appealing product descriptions, engaging representations, and an online presence that speaks to the artistic value of your creations. Your portfolio becomes a testament to the synergy between human creativity and the augmenting power of AI.

As your artistic endeavors take shape, explore strategies for navigating online artistic marketplaces. Gemini AI becomes your strategic partner in reaching a global audience that appreciates the unique fusion of art and technology. From established platforms to independent storefronts, leverage Gemini AI's insights to position your creations for maximum visibility and income potential.

Data Analysis and Reporting Services

In the era of information, data holds the key to unlocking insights and driving informed decisions. Enter the realm where Google Gemini AI becomes a formidable ally, transforming raw data into actionable intelligence. This section explores how Gemini AI's data processing capabilities can be harnessed to analyze data and generate comprehensive reports, catering to the needs of businesses and research institutions.

Witness the transformative power of Gemini AI as it steps into the realm of data processing. Explore how this sophisticated AI system becomes your trusted companion in navigating the vast seas of information, revolutionizing the way businesses and research institutions harness the potential hidden within their datasets.

For businesses seeking a competitive edge, Gemini AI becomes the catalyst for market intelligence. Dive into the capabilities of data analysis, where Gemini AI not only interprets market trends but also predicts future trajectories. Businesses can leverage this intelligence to make strategic decisions, optimize operations, and stay ahead in the dynamic landscape of their respective industries.

Explore how Gemini AI generates insights that go beyond mere data interpretation. Decision-makers in businesses and research institutions can rely on Gemini AI to provide strategic insights, allowing them to foresee challenges, identify opportunities, and make decisions that are backed by the power of data-driven intelligence.

Gemini AI excels in translating complex data sets into comprehensible reports. Discover how businesses can benefit from customized reporting, tailored to their specific needs. Gemini AI ensures that the generated reports not only convey the data effectively but also offer actionable recommendations, empowering businesses to implement strategies for growth and success.

In the realm of research institutions, Gemini AI becomes an invaluable asset for scientific data analysis. Uncover how this AI system enhances the efficiency of data interpretation, supporting researchers in their quest for discoveries. Whether in healthcare, academia, or scientific research, Gemini AI's data processing capabilities elevate the standards of analysis and contribute to groundbreaking findings.

Gemini AI goes beyond static analysis; it automates data processing workflows. Explore how businesses and research institutions can save time and resources by entrusting repetitive data tasks to Gemini AI. This not only improves efficiency but also allows human resources to focus on high-level decision-making and creative problem-solving.

As businesses and research institutions delve into the realm of data analysis with Gemini AI, it's essential to address the aspects of data security and ethics. This section delves into the measures and considerations that should be taken to ensure the responsible and ethical use of data in alignment with industry standards and regulations.

Positioning yourself as an expert in data analysis and reporting, offering valuable services

In the dynamic landscape of data-driven decision-making, positioning yourself as an expert in data analysis and reporting is not just a strategic move—it's a pathway to becoming an indispensable asset in the business and research domains. This section unveils the steps to establish your expertise, leveraging Google Gemini AI's data processing capabilities to offer valuable services that set you apart in the realm of data analytics.

Become the author of your expertise story. Explore how Gemini AI can assist in crafting a narrative that communicates your proficiency in data analysis. From highlighting your skill set to showcasing past successes, this section guides you through the process of presenting yourself as a seasoned professional with a unique blend of analytical prowess and technological finesse.

Every expert needs a portfolio that speaks volumes about their capabilities. Discover how Gemini AI aids in curating a portfolio that goes beyond mere data points. Whether it's business success stories, research milestones, or innovative data-driven solutions, Gemini AI becomes your ally in showcasing a comprehensive portfolio that resonates with potential clients and collaborators.

In the digital age, your online presence is your business card. Learn how Gemini AI can contribute to building a compelling online presence. From crafting a professional bio to optimizing your LinkedIn profile, Gemini AI ensures that your expertise is not only conveyed effectively but also reaches the right audience, positioning you as a thought leader in the field of data analysis.

Thought leadership is not just about what you know but how effectively you communicate it. Dive into the strategies of content creation, where Gemini AI becomes your content collaborator. From blog posts to industry insights, explore how Gemini AI aids in generating content that establishes your authority in data analysis, setting the stage for thought leadership.

Positioning yourself as an expert goes beyond individual accomplishments. Uncover how Gemini AI can assist in identifying networking opportunities and potential collaborations. Whether it's connecting with industry peers, participating in webinars, or collaborating on research projects, Gemini AI becomes your strategic partner in expanding your network and solidifying your position as a go-to expert in data analytics.

Gemini AI's data processing capabilities allow for the creation of tailored services that cater to specific business and research needs. Explore how you can leverage this capability to offer customized solutions. Whether it's creating specialized data reports, conducting in-depth analyses, or providing strategic consultation, Gemini AI ensures that your services are not just valuable but indispensable in the data-driven landscape.

In the ever-evolving field of data analytics, staying ahead requires continuous learning and adaptation. Uncover how Gemini AI can assist in keeping you updated on the latest trends, technologies, and methodologies. From recommending relevant courses to providing insights on emerging tools, Gemini AI becomes your learning companion, ensuring that your expertise remains cutting-edge.

Chapter 6:

Tips for Success with Gemini AI

Focus on Value

In the world of data analytics, the true measure of success isn't just in deciphering complex datasets but in solving real-world problems and delivering genuine value to your target audience. This section explores the pivotal role of Google Gemini AI in ensuring that your data expertise goes beyond numbers, creating meaningful solutions that address tangible challenges and resonate with the needs of your audience.

Step into the realm where data meets humanity. Explore how Gemini AI assists in understanding the human element within datasets. Beyond statistical patterns, Gemini AI helps unearth the stories behind the numbers—real challenges faced by individuals, businesses, and research institutions. This understanding becomes the cornerstone for crafting data-driven solutions that are not just accurate but deeply impactful.

Gemini AI becomes your detective in the data landscape, uncovering pain points and challenges faced by your target audience. Whether it's business inefficiencies, research roadblocks, or societal issues, Gemini AI's analytical capabilities provide insights that go beyond surface-level observations. Identifying these challenges becomes the foundation for offering solutions that genuinely address the needs of your audience.

Discover how Gemini AI transforms data insights into tailored solutions. By analyzing patterns, trends, and outliers, Gemini AI aids in the creation of customized strategies that directly address the identified challenges. These solutions are not generic; they are precise, effective, and tailored to meet the specific needs of your audience, ensuring that your expertise translates into real-world impact.

Gemini AI plays a pivotal role in ensuring that data applications are user-centric. Whether it's a business dashboard, a research tool, or a societal intervention, Gemini AI contributes to designing applications that prioritize user experience. The result is not just functional solutions but intuitive and user-friendly applications that resonate with the end-users, offering genuine value in their day-to-day operations.

Communication is key in translating data insights into actionable solutions. Explore how Gemini AI assists in enhancing transparency in your data-driven processes. From explaining complex analyses to providing clear recommendations, Gemini AI becomes your communication ally, ensuring that your solutions are not only effective but also understood and embraced by your target audience.

Gemini AI's analytics capabilities extend beyond initial insights. Delve into how Gemini AI aids in measuring the impact of implemented solutions. By analyzing ongoing data, you can assess the effectiveness of your strategies and iterate based on real-time feedback. This iterative approach ensures that your data expertise remains dynamic, responsive, and continuously aligned with the evolving needs of your audience.

Finally, explore how Gemini AI helps in demonstrating the value of your data expertise beyond mere numerical outputs. Whether it's showcasing cost savings, efficiency improvements, or societal impact, Gemini AI contributes to framing the narrative that emphasizes the real-world value generated by your data-driven solutions.

Demonstrating how genuine value creation leads to sustained success

Embarking on the journey of sustained success in the realm of data analytics is not just about delivering solutions—it's about creating genuine value that becomes the bedrock of your enduring triumph. In this section, discover how Google Gemini AI plays a pivotal role in translating value creation into sustained success, ensuring that your expertise becomes synonymous with long-term impact and prosperity.

Discover how creating genuine value with Gemini AI becomes the cornerstone of building enduring relationships. By consistently offering solutions that address real challenges, you foster trust and loyalty among your audience. These relationships go beyond individual projects, forming the basis of long-term collaborations and partnerships that contribute to sustained success in the dynamic landscape of data analytics.

In the fast-paced world of data analytics, staying relevant is paramount. Explore how Gemini AI assists in monitoring industry trends and adapting your strategies accordingly. By leveraging Gemini AI's insights, you can anticipate shifts in the data landscape, positioning yourself ahead of the curve. This proactive approach ensures that your expertise evolves with the industry, contributing to sustained success.

Sustained success is not static; it's dynamic, requiring a continuous cycle of measurement and adaptation. Dive into how Gemini AI aids in measuring the impact of your solutions over time. By analyzing ongoing data, you can identify areas of improvement, iterate on your strategies, and ensure that your data expertise remains effective and aligned with the evolving needs of your audience.

Genuine value creation is not a one-time feat—it's a consistent commitment. Explore how Gemini AI becomes your ally in demonstrating consistent value through various projects. Whether it's optimizing business processes, contributing to groundbreaking research, or addressing societal challenges, Gemini AI ensures that your track record of value creation becomes a testament to your sustained success.

Elevate your status from a data expert to a thought leader in the field. Uncover how Gemini AI contributes to your thought leadership journey. By consistently delivering valuable insights, thought-provoking analyses, and innovative solutions, you position yourself as a go-to authority in the data analytics landscape. This positioning not only attracts new opportunities but also cements your status as a key influencer, paving the way for sustained success.

Sustained success is not just about what you achieve but how you achieve it. Delve into how Gemini AI aids in upholding ethical standards in your data analytics endeavors. By ensuring compliance with industry ethics and data privacy regulations, you build a reputation for integrity and responsibility. This commitment to ethical practices becomes a pillar supporting your sustained success in the long run.

Explore how Gemini AI contributes to scaling the impact of your data expertise. By automating repetitive tasks and streamlining processes, Gemini AI allows you to expand your reach and take on larger projects. This scalability not only contributes to sustained success but also positions you as a versatile expert capable of handling diverse challenges in the expansive landscape of data analytics

Quality over Quantity

In the transformative landscape of AI-powered endeavors, the pursuit of excellence is not an option—it's a necessity. This section delves into the critical importance of prioritizing the quality of your AI outputs when harnessing the capabilities of Google Gemini AI. Discover how a commitment to excellence becomes the linchpin of your success, ensuring that every AI-generated output is not just a product but a testament to your dedication to precision, reliability, and innovation.

Uncover how prioritizing the quality of your AI outputs with Gemini AI begins with an unwavering commitment to precision. Whether it's generating content, crafting code snippets, or analyzing data, Gemini AI's capabilities are harnessed to produce outputs that are not just accurate but reflect a standard of precision that sets you apart in the competitive landscape. This commitment to precision becomes the foundation for building trust and reliability among your audience.

Explore how Gemini AI becomes your collaborator in refining content creation. From blog posts to marketing copy, Gemini AI aids in the creation of outputs that go beyond mere information—they embody clarity, coherence, and engagement. The focus on quality ensures that every piece of content resonates with your audience, establishing you as a content creator who values substance as much as style.

In the realm of code generation, excellence is synonymous with quality and reliability. Dive into how Gemini AI contributes to ensuring that the code snippets and scripts it generates adhere to industry standards. The emphasis on quality extends beyond functionality to encompass readability, efficiency, and adaptability. This commitment to code quality positions you as a developer who not only embraces automation but also upholds the highest standards of coding practices.

Quality isn't just about numbers; it's about the insights derived from them. Learn how Gemini AI aids in elevating the quality of data analysis and reporting. From uncovering meaningful patterns to presenting clear and actionable insights, Gemini AI ensures that your data outputs transcend raw data points. This elevation in quality transforms your data analyses into strategic assets that contribute to informed decision-making.

Examine how Gemini AI becomes your ally in the continuous process of proofreading and refinement. Regardless of the output—be it content, code, or data analyses—Gemini AI's capabilities are harnessed for ongoing refinement. This commitment to constant improvement ensures that every AI-generated output undergoes scrutiny, leading to outputs that are not just good but continually strive for excellence.

Quality isn't sacrificed in the pursuit of automation; instead, it's enhanced through strategic human oversight. Discover how Gemini AI allows for a balanced approach, where automation expedites processes while human judgment ensures the quality of outputs. This synergy ensures that AI-generated outputs embody the best of both worlds—efficiency and precision guided by human expertise.

Quality isn't just a feature; it's a brand. Delve into how prioritizing the quality of your AI outputs with Gemini AI contributes to establishing a reputation for excellence. From garnering positive reviews to building trust among clients and collaborators, the consistent delivery of high-quality outputs becomes a hallmark of your brand. This reputation not only attracts new opportunities but also cements your position as a leader in the AI-powered landscape.

Tips on proofreading content, refining code, and ensuring polished and professional offerings

In the dynamic landscape of AI-powered content creation, code generation, and data analysis, the journey to excellence doesn't end with the initial output. This section unveils essential tips for proofreading content, refining code, and ensuring that your offerings stand out as polished and professional with the assistance of Google Gemini AI. Let's dive into the strategies that elevate your outputs from good to exceptional.

1. Content Proofreading Mastery:

- **Leverage Gemini AI for Initial Drafts:** Use Gemini AI's natural language processing to generate initial drafts of content. These drafts serve as a foundation for your proofreading process, saving time and providing a starting point for refinement.

- **Contextual Understanding:** Gemini AI's contextual understanding capabilities ensure that generated content aligns with the intended message. During proofreading, focus on ensuring that the context is maintained and that the content seamlessly flows, providing a cohesive reading experience.

- **Grammar and Style Checks:** Gemini AI's grammar and style checks are valuable proofreading assistants. Pay attention to suggestions provided by the AI, refining sentence structures, correcting grammar issues, and ensuring adherence to the desired writing style.

- **Human Touch:** While Gemini AI aids in content generation, your unique voice and perspective remain crucial. Infuse a human touch during proofreading by adding personal insights, anecdotes, or industry-specific nuances that enhance the authenticity of the content.

2. Code Refinement Excellence:

- **Automated Code Generation:** Utilize Gemini AI for automated code generation, saving time and effort. The AI can swiftly provide code snippets based on your requirements.

- **Readability and Comments:** During code refinement, prioritize readability. Gemini AI can assist in adding comments and improving the structure of generated code. Ensure that the code is not only functional but also comprehensible to other developers.

- **Error Handling:** Gemini AI's capabilities extend to error handling in code. Use the AI to identify potential issues, refine error messages, and enhance the robustness of the code.

- **Optimization Suggestions:** Gemini AI provides optimization suggestions for code snippets. Consider these suggestions during refinement to ensure that the code is efficient, adhering to best practices in programming.

3. Polishing Professional Offerings:

- **Visual Appeal:** For content-rich websites or marketing materials, Gemini AI can contribute to the visual appeal. Proofread and refine the layout and formatting suggested by the AI to ensure a polished and professional look.

- **Consistent Branding:** Whether it's content, code, or data reports, maintain consistent branding. Gemini AI can assist in aligning the tone and style with your brand guidelines, contributing to a cohesive and professional identity.

- **Data Visualization Refinement:** If your offerings involve data analysis and reporting, leverage Gemini AI for data visualization suggestions. Refine the charts, graphs, and visual elements to enhance clarity and professionalism.

- **Client-Centric Language:** During the proofreading process, ensure that the language used in client-facing materials is client-centric. Gemini AI can assist in tailoring language to resonate with your target audience, contributing to a more professional tone.

4. Iterative Refinement:

- **Feedback Incorporation:** If you receive feedback from clients or collaborators, use Gemini AI for iterative refinement. Implement suggestions, refine content or code accordingly, and ensure that your offerings continuously evolve based on real-world feedback.

- **Continuous Improvement Mindset:** Approach proofreading, refinement, and polishing as a continuous improvement process. Gemini AI's capabilities allow for iterative enhancements, ensuring that your outputs are always on the cutting edge of quality and professionalism.

Stay Updated and Adapt

In the ever-evolving landscape of artificial intelligence, staying ahead requires a commitment to continuous learning. Explore the profound impact of keeping pace with Gemini AI's latest features and capabilities. Discover how embracing a learning mindset can propel you to the forefront of innovation and expertise within the dynamic realm of Google's Gemini AI.

1. Navigating New Frontiers:

- **Platform Exploration Routine:** Regularly delve into the Gemini AI platform. Discover new features and functionalities by navigating through its interface. Familiarity with the platform's nuances not only enhances your user experience but also unveils hidden capabilities that can transform your AI-powered endeavors.

- **Stay Informed with Release Notes:** Keep a watchful eye on release notes and updates provided by Google for Gemini AI. These documents serve as your compass through the evolving landscape, highlighting the introduction of novel features, performance improvements, and valuable bug fixes.

2. Mastering Advanced Capabilities:

- **Tap into User Guides:** Harness the wealth of information within advanced user guides and documentation. These resources are treasure troves that provide in-depth insights into Gemini AI's advanced capabilities. Invest time in studying these guides to unlock the full potential of the AI system and integrate advanced features seamlessly.

- **Online Tutorials and Courses:** Enrich your understanding by exploring online tutorials and courses dedicated to Gemini AI. Google's learning resources and third-party educational platforms offer courses that delve into advanced functionalities. Immerse yourself in these courses to gain practical insights and hands-on experience.

3. Community Synergy:

- **Engage in User Forums:** Join user forums and online communities where fellow enthusiasts share knowledge and experiences related to Gemini AI. Participating in discussions exposes you to diverse perspectives, innovative use cases, and real-world applications.

- **Attend Webinars and Virtual Events:** Actively participate in webinars and virtual events hosted by Google or AI-related organizations. These platforms serve as dynamic arenas where the latest features, updates, and best practices for Gemini AI are unveiled. Take advantage of Q&A sessions to glean insights from industry experts.

4. Hands-On Experimentation:

- Create Learning Projects: Set aside dedicated time for hands-on experimentation. Create learning projects or sandbox environments where you can freely explore new features and functionalities. This practical approach allows you to test, iterate, and uncover inventive ways to apply Gemini AI's capabilities.

- Contribute to Open Source: Extend your learning by contributing to open source projects related to Gemini AI. Collaborating with the community on shared initiatives not only broadens your exposure to diverse perspectives but also allows you to work on cutting-edge projects that push the boundaries of what is achievable with Gemini AI.

5. Network of Professionals:

- **Forge Professional Connections:** Build and foster professional networks within the AI and machine learning community. Connections with industry peers offer opportunities to exchange insights, stay informed about emerging trends, and access collective knowledge that transcends individual learning efforts.

- **Explore Mentorship Opportunities:** Seek mentorship within the AI community. Mentor-mentee relationships provide structured guidance, allowing you to navigate

Gemini AI's features and capabilities with the wisdom gained from practical experience.

6. Certification Pathway:

- **Pursue Official Certifications:** Consider pursuing official certifications offered by Google for Gemini AI. Certification programs not only validate your expertise but also provide a structured curriculum for continuous learning. Achieving certifications ensures you stay well-versed in the latest features and best practices.

- **Renew and Refresh:** If certifications have expiration dates, commit to continuous renewal. This process involves updating your knowledge to align with the latest features and requirements, reinforcing your dedication to staying current in the ever-evolving field of AI.

In the ever-evolving landscape of AI-powered passive income, the ability to adapt stands as the linchpin between stagnation and success. Let's delve into the pivotal role of adaptability in optimizing income-generating strategies and how it becomes the guiding force in navigating the dynamic currents of the digital era.

1. The Dynamic Nature of the Digital Landscape: In the realm of AI-powered passive income, change is the only constant. Algorithms evolve, consumer behaviors shift, and market trends undergo metamorphosis. To harness the full potential of income-generating strategies, one must acknowledge and embrace the dynamic nature of the digital landscape.

2. Responsive Strategy Iteration: Adaptability manifests in the art of responsive strategy iteration. Income strategies should not be etched in stone but rather treated as living blueprints subject to refinement. Regularly reassessing and tweaking strategies based on the latest insights ensures they remain aligned with the ever-changing demands of the digital ecosystem.

3. Agility in Content Creation: The heartbeat of passive income often lies in content creation. An adaptable content strategy responds to audience feedback, embraces emerging formats, and aligns with the current preferences of consumers. Whether it's adjusting the tone, format, or delivery, adaptability ensures that content continues to resonate and engage effectively.

4. Diversification in Monetization: The adaptability principle extends to monetization avenues. Income streams should not be monolithic but rather a diversified portfolio. If one avenue faces saturation or shifts in consumer interest, having alternative monetization channels allows for a seamless transition, maintaining financial stability.

5. Leverage Emerging Technologies: As technology advances, new opportunities arise. The adaptable individual seizes these opportunities, leveraging emerging technologies to augment income strategies. Whether integrating augmented reality, exploring new platforms, or harnessing the power of the latest AI features, adaptability ensures staying at the forefront of innovation.

6.   Consumer-Centric   Approach: Adaptability in income generation entails a deep understanding of consumer needs and preferences. Strategies should pivot in response to shifts in consumer behavior, ensuring that products or services provided remain relevant and valuable. This consumer-centric adaptability fosters sustained customer loyalty and trust.

7. Agile Marketing Campaigns: Digital marketing, a cornerstone of passive income, demands agile campaigns. Adaptable marketing strategies respond swiftly to changes in algorithms, market dynamics, and consumer trends. This agility not only safeguards against obsolescence but positions income generators to capitalize on emerging opportunities.

8. Data-Driven Decision Making: Adaptability thrives in a data-driven environment. Regular analysis of performance metrics, consumer data, and market trends empowers individuals to make informed decisions. This adaptability fueled by insights ensures that strategies are not based on assumptions but grounded in the ever-shifting realities of the digital landscape.

9. Future-Proofing: The truly adaptable not only respond to the present but also prepare for the future. Anticipating trends, staying informed about technological advancements, and proactively adjusting strategies to align with foreseeable shifts contribute to the long-term sustainability of income-generating endeavors.

Build a Community:

In the expansive realm of AI-powered passive income, forging connections isn't just a strategy; it's the heartbeat of sustainable success. Let's explore the art of engagement, delving into the importance of connecting with potential clients and fellow AI enthusiasts to nurture relationships and fuel collaborative growth.

1. Establishing a Digital Presence:
Begin the engagement journey by establishing a robust digital presence. A well-crafted online persona across platforms – be it social media, forums, or professional networks – serves as the initial handshake in the vast digital landscape.

2.   Authentic   Conversations:
Engagement transcends mere interaction; it's about authentic conversations. Strive for meaningful dialogues that go beyond superficial exchanges. Share insights, ask probing questions, and contribute to discussions in a way that adds value to the community.

3. Tailoring Content for Engagement:
Craft content with engagement in mind.

Whether it's blog posts, social media updates, or interactive polls, tailor your content to spark conversations. Pose thought-provoking questions, share personal experiences, and encourage your audience to share their perspectives.

4. Participate in Communities: Join AI-centric communities and forums where potential clients and enthusiasts gather. Actively participate in discussions, share your expertise, and learn from the experiences of others. It's within these digital congregations that valuable connections are often forged.

5. Networking Events and Webinars: Attend virtual networking events and webinars dedicated to AI and passive income. These platforms provide a stage for engaging with like-minded individuals, potential clients, and industry experts. Network, share your experiences, and be open to collaborations that might emerge from these interactions.

6. Respond Promptly: In the fast-paced digital sphere, prompt responsiveness is a virtue. Whether it's responding to comments on your content or replying to direct messages, swift and thoughtful responses demonstrate your commitment to engagement and build a positive rapport.

7. Showcasing Expertise: Position yourself as an authority in your niche by showcasing your expertise. Share case studies, success stories, and insights that highlight your proficiency in AI-powered passive income. This not only attracts potential clients but also fosters credibility within the enthusiast community.

8. Collaborative Projects: Explore collaborative projects with fellow AI enthusiasts. Whether it's co-authoring articles, conducting joint webinars, or initiating shared ventures, collaboration amplifies your reach and brings diverse skill sets to the table.

9. Building Trust Through Consistency: Engagement is a journey, not a destination. Consistency is key to building trust over time. Regularly contribute valuable content, engage in conversations, and demonstrate reliability in your interactions. Trust is the bedrock upon which lasting relationships are constructed.

10. Attend AI Conferences and Meetups: Participate in AI conferences and meetups, whether in person or virtually. These events provide opportunities for face-to-face interactions, networking, and establishing a more personal connection with potential clients and fellow enthusiasts.

In the dynamic realm of AI-powered passive income, networking emerges as the catalyst for unlocking a plethora of possibilities. Let's delve into the art of networking, where sharing expertise becomes the currency and building trust acts as the foundation for attracting customers and opportunities.

1. Strategic Networking Platforms: Identify and strategically position yourself on networking platforms where potential clients and opportunities abound. Platforms like LinkedIn, industry forums, and virtual meetups serve as fertile grounds for connecting with like-minded individuals.

2. Expertise as a Magnet: Your expertise is your magnetic force. Share your insights, experiences, and knowledge in a way that captivates your audience. Whether through blog posts, social media updates, or forum discussions, position yourself as a valuable resource in the AI-powered passive income landscape.

3. Elevate Others: Networking is a two-way street. Actively seek opportunities to elevate others in your network. Share their content, acknowledge their achievements, and contribute to their success. This reciprocity fosters a positive ecosystem where collaboration becomes a natural outcome.

4. Thought Leadership: Become a thought leader in your niche. Regularly publish content that challenges conventional thinking, offers innovative solutions, and demonstrates a deep understanding of the AI landscape. Thought leadership not only attracts customers but positions you as a go-to figure for opportunities.

5. Authentic Connections: Authenticity is the cornerstone of effective networking.

Be genuine in your interactions, share both successes and challenges, and allow your personality to shine through. Authentic connections form the bedrock of trust, a crucial element in attracting long-term customers.

6. Engage in Conversations: Don't just be a passive presence in your network; actively engage in conversations. Respond to comments on your content, join discussions, and initiate dialogues. Engagement fosters a sense of community and positions you at the forefront of relevant conversations.

7. Case Studies and Success Stories: Share real-world case studies and success stories that highlight the tangible impact of AI-powered passive income. Case studies not only serve as testimonials but also showcase your ability to deliver results, making you an attractive prospect for potential customers.

8. Build Trust Through Consistency: Consistency is the glue that binds networking efforts. Regularly contribute to the conversation, share valuable content, and deliver on promises. Trust is cultivated over time through a consistent demonstration of reliability and authenticity.

9. Personal Branding: Craft a compelling personal brand that resonates with your target audience. Your brand is not just about visuals; it's about the story you tell, the values you embody, and the promises you uphold. A strong personal brand becomes a beacon that attracts customers and opportunities.

10. Attend Industry Events: Participate in industry events, conferences, and webinars to expand your network beyond digital platforms. Face-to-face interactions create lasting impressions and open doors to a myriad of opportunities.

Conclusion

As our journey through the realms of AI-powered passive income with Google Gemini AI draws to a close, the narrative we've unfolded reveals a tapestry of opportunities and promises. Let's weave the concluding chapter, summarizing the odyssey we've embarked on and casting a vision for the readers' own transformative experience in the world of automated income.

Picture this: Google Gemini AI, a technological marvel standing at the intersection of natural language processing, machine learning, and data analysis. It's not just a tool; it's the key that unlocks doors to diverse income streams, reshaping the landscape of passive earnings.

Our journey ventured into the expansive territories of content creation, digital marketing, and customer service, illustrating the vast array of possibilities that Gemini AI presents. Monetization strategies unfolded like a tapestry—each thread weaving a story of potential, innovation, and financial prosperity.

In the ever-evolving landscape of AI, the mantra for success reverberates with adaptability. As the technological canvas continues to unfold, the ability to pivot strategies, embrace change, and stay ahead of the curve becomes the compass guiding us towards sustained success.

But success is not solitary; it's a collaborative masterpiece. Networking and engaging with clients and AI enthusiasts emerged as the brushstrokes that add vibrancy to our narrative. Trust, expertise, and authenticity became the ink that etched meaningful connections in the vast parchment of the digital world.

As we stand at the crossroads of our AI-powered odyssey, the horizon shimmers with promises. The potential for automated income flows like a river, and financial freedom is not a distant shore but a destination waiting to be explored.

Dear reader, the adventure does not end here. I extend an invitation—an invitation to explore the possibilities that Google Gemini AI holds for you. Dive into the stream of automated income, where the currents of innovation and strategic deployment of AI technologies guide your vessel.

Our concluding chapter is not just an epilogue; it's a prelude to a future where automated income is not a dream but a reality. As you embark on your own odyssey, be at the vanguard of the automated income revolution. Let the possibilities be your guiding stars and the future, a canvas waiting for the strokes of your creative endeavors.

In this narrative of AI-powered dreams, you're not just a reader; you're the protagonist, and the story unfolds with every strategic decision, innovative choice, and collaborative endeavor. May your AI-powered journey be filled with the resonance of success and the melody of financial freedom, as you become the storyteller of your own transformative tale.